IMAGES
of Rail

RAILROADS OF PLACER COUNTY

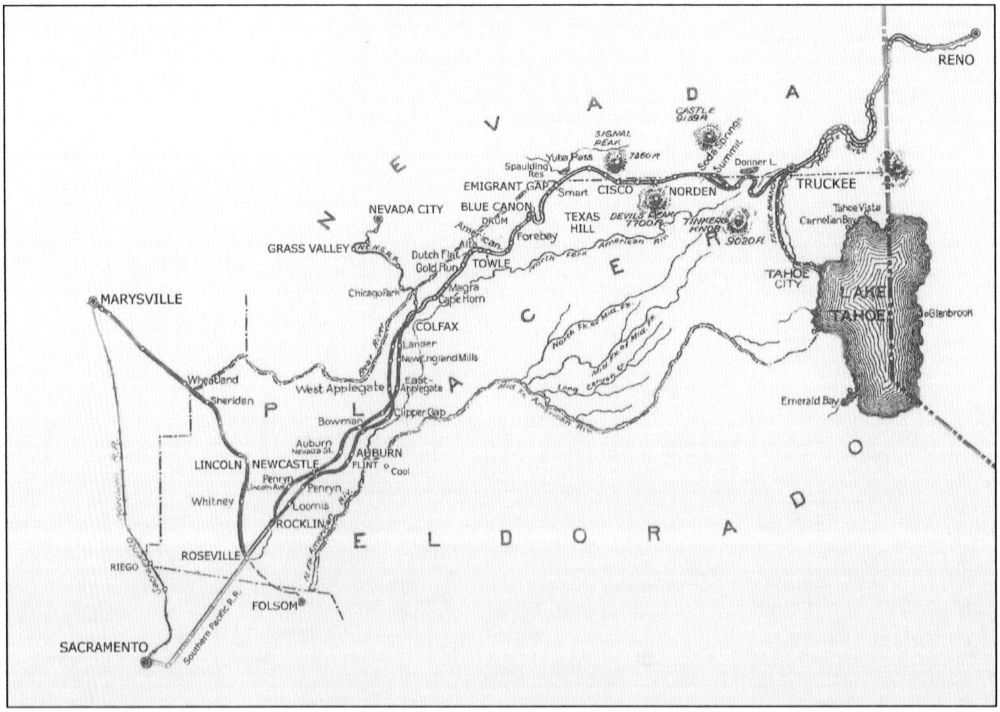

This map shows some of the railroads that operated in Placer County, California, around 1920. Placer County is sandwiched between Nevada County on the north and El Dorado County on the south. The state of Nevada and Reno are to the right of the heavy dotted vertical line that cuts through Lake Tahoe. The detailed railroad routes and place-names were extracted from a Sacramento Division–Southern Pacific (SP) Railroad map dated 1919. The appearance of two lines for the railroad between Rocklin and Colfax resulted when SP double-tracked the route as described in chapter 3. Most of the SP route over Donner Summit from Sacramento to Truckee fell within the boundaries of Placer County, as did part of the SP route between Sacramento and Marysville. The Nevada County Narrow Gauge Railroad (NCNG) and the Lake Tahoe Railway linked stations in Placer County and adjacent Nevada County. Also identified on the map are many of the key locations mentioned in the chapters on Sacramento Northern, Mountain Quarries, Towle Brothers, and Pacific Gas & Electric Railroads. The dotted line between Folsom and Roseville was added to represent the approximate route of the 1860s California Central Railroad, which is discussed in chapter 1 along with other early Placer County railroads. (Map modifications by Roger Staab.)

On the Cover: This scene in Colfax from the 1880s shows an NCNG train with its tender filled with wood waiting at the Central Pacific Railroad (CPRR) passenger depot. The Colfax Depot was shared by the NCNG and the CPRR, with the NCNG tracks on the far side of the platform and the CPRR tracks on the near side. The building beyond the train is the Central Hotel. An expanded view of this early Colfax scene can be found on page 89. (Arthur Sommers.)

IMAGES
of Rail

RAILROADS OF PLACER COUNTY

Arthur Sommers and Roger Staab

ARCADIA
PUBLISHING

ISBN 978-1-4671-2764-6

Published by Arcadia Publishing
Charleston, South Carolina

Printed in the United States of America

Library of Congress Control Number: 2017958427

For all general information, please contact Arcadia Publishing:
Telephone 843-853-2070
Fax 843-853-0044
E-mail sales@arcadiapublishing.com
For customer service and orders:
Toll-Free 1-888-313-2665

Visit us on the Internet at www.arcadiapublishing.com

In this view offering a look into an eastbound Southern Pacific dining car, the Placer County Courthouse at Auburn is in the background. (Arthur Sommers.)

Contents

Acknowledgments

We would like to acknowledge the people and organizations below for their assistance in the preparation of this book.

Chuck Spinks and Tony Hesch provided technical review comments on an early draft of the book. Andrew Brandon provided technical review comments and some photographs from his collection. Rodi Lee, Carmel Barry-Schweyer, and Margaret Hubber reviewed early drafts and provided comments to us. Allen Fisher provided images from the Western Railroad Museum for use in chapter 4. Dana Scanlon provided images from his personal collection for use in chapter 9.

Local railroad historian Ken Yeo provided many of the images used in chapter 6 as well as some of the Alfred Hart photographs from his collection, which appear in chapter 2. These are cited as (Alfred Hart/Ken Yeo). Other Hart images appearing in chapter 2 were obtained from the Stanford University online library, cited as (Alfred Hart/Stanford) in the captions. The complete citation is "Alfred A. Hart Photographs (PC0002). Department of Special Collections, Stanford University Libraries."

The Placer-Sierra Railroad Heritage Society (cited as PSRHS) provided several photographs from its collection.

Images from author Arthur Sommers's collection are identified as (AJS).

Research Sources:

Best, Gerald. *Nevada County Narrow Gauge*. Burbank, CA: Howell-North, 1965.

Diebert, Timothy and Joseph Strapac. *Southern Pacific Steam Locomotive Compendium*. Huntington Beach, CA: Shade Tree, 1987.

Drew, Stephen E. *Lake Tahoe's Railroads*. Charleston, SC: Arcadia Publishing, 2016.

Dunscomb, Guy. *A Century of Southern Pacific Steam Locomotives*. San Jose: Train Shop, 1963.

Lee, Rodi and Michael G. Lynch. *American River Canyon*. Charleston, SC: Arcadia Publishing, 2012.

McKeon, Owen F. *The Railroads and Steamers of Lake Tahoe*. San Mateo, CA: Western Railroader.

Signor, John. *Donner Pass: Southern Pacific's Sierra Crossing*. San Marino, CA: Golden West, 1985.

Thompson & West. *History of Placer County, California, with Illustrations and Biographical Sketches of Its Prominent Men and Pioneers*. Oakland, CA: Pacific Press, 1882.

Trimble, Paul C. *Sacramento Northern Railway*. Charleston, SC: Arcadia Publishing, 2005.

Roger Staab's shares of the proceeds from the sale of this book have been assigned to Placer-Sierra Railroad Heritage Society (www.psrhs.org) to help fund its historic preservation efforts.

INTRODUCTION

Railroads began to develop and expand in eastern portions of the United States in the early 1800s. Most were concentrated in populated areas or in regions with abundant natural resources such as coal or iron ore. The railroads soon proved to be a profitable way to move people and goods with greater speed and efficiency than with horse- or oxen-drawn wagons or coaches.

How then did railroads migrate to the West Coast and the new state of California? And why were the new rail lines concentrated in certain areas of the state, such as Placer County? To help answer those questions, the following provides some background on California's formative years.

In 1845, the United States annexed Texas, which was considered by Mexico at that time to still be part of its territory. This annexation precipitated a war (1846–1848) between Mexico and the United States. The peace treaty signed between the two warring nations was called the Treaty of Guadalupe Hidalgo and was signed on February 8, 1848. Mexico lost the war and ceded its northern territories of what would become California, Texas, Nevada, Arizona, New Mexico, Utah, and parts of Colorado to the United States for $15 million (1848 dollars). In January 1848, gold was discovered at Coloma on the South Fork of the American River in Northern California. This discovery of gold started the famous California Gold Rush, with fortune hunters flooding in from all over the world. Imagine how different the history of North America would have evolved if Mexico had not lost the war so quickly and had still possessed California when gold was discovered in January 1848, only a month before Mexico signed the peace treaty.

The discovery of gold and the movement of people into California was the impetus for California being accepted into the Union as the 31st state. California identified 27 original counties when first admitted into the Union in 1850. Only a year later, the influx of thousands of people looking to make their fortunes caused the California legislature to break up some of the original counties and form new counties from the pieces. Smaller counties were needed to allow a better span of control over county business by county officials. Placer County was one of those newly formed counties in 1851. Today, there are 58 counties in California.

Though Placer County is relatively small in size—1,506 square miles, less than one percent of all of California—that area ended up being home to numerous different railroads over the years. Some of those railroads were standard gauge, some were narrow gauge, some were long, and some were very short. Several more were proposed but never built. Increasingly, people, goods, and mining and construction materials needed to be transported to and from nearby or remote mines, mills, and settlements. Proposed new railroads attracted investors and their newfound wealth, but building a railroad was not easy in those early days. Locomotives, rails, and other supplies had to be transported from the eastern states to California via ships sailing around Cape Horn or across the Isthmus of Panama. By the 1860s, there was a growing need for a railroad connecting remote California and the rest of the nation to move goods and people faster across the great expanse of the central plains and western mountains. Along with being rich in timber and mining resources, Placer County found itself on the preferred route of the nation's first transcontinental railroad.

This book provides the reader with a short history of 14 of Placer County's railroads. Some of the earliest railroads were short-lived, and few images exist of those early lines. Others were like the Central Pacific Railroad, which had hundreds of images taken even during its earliest days of construction because it was the western end of the first transcontinental railroad connecting the East with the West and as such drew a lot of attention.

Though Placer County is small in size compared to the rest of California, its location led to a disproportionate share of railroad construction and operations. Placer County was at the heart of much of the early gold mining and the growth of mining towns in the mid to late 1800s, and one of its mountain ridges became the favored route over the Sierra Nevada for the nation's first transcontinental railroad. (PSRHS.)

One

Early Railroads

This first chapter covers the history of three different, early Placer County railroads—the California Central Railroad, the Yuba Railroad Company, and the Sacramento, Placer & Nevada Railroad.

The California Central Railroad Company was incorporated on April 21, 1857, and ran a five-foot-gauge line on a single track between Folsom in Sacramento County and Lincoln in Placer County. That short line was completed on October 31, 1861. By April 26, 1864, the Central Pacific Railroad opened a line from Sacramento to Roseville, where it crossed the California Central Railroad. At that time, Roseville was appropriately called Junction. On July 22, 1868, the California Central Railroad was foreclosed, and its existing operations were purchased by the California & Oregon Railroad. The California & Oregon Railroad soon came to be operated by the Central Pacific Railroad and was consolidated under the CPRR name on August 22, 1870. On that date, the Central Pacific owned 77.53 miles of track heading north out of Lincoln. There were 23.90 miles acquired with the absorption of the Yuba Railroad Company, 10.30 miles of the former California Central Railroad, plus 43.33 miles between Marysville and Chico constructed between May and July 1870. The California Central Railroad, the Yuba Railroad Company, the Sacramento, Placer & Nevada Railroad, and the Central Pacific Railroad (see chapter 2) were all operating in Placer County during the Civil War years of 1861–1865.

The Yuba Railroad Company incorporated in 1862 with the objective of extending the tracks laid by the California Central Railroad farther north from Lincoln. By 1867, the line was opened from Lincoln in Placer County to Wheatland in Yuba County. Marysville was reached in 1869. The Yuba Railroad Company was absorbed by the California & Oregon Railroad Company in 1869. All the early railroads being built on the West Coast, including those in Placer County, had to have the rails shipped from the East Coast either around Cape Horn or across the Isthmus of Panama. The first rails were made of iron. There was no company on the West Coast with a capability to manufacture rails in the early years. The much better steel rails were not made in abundance in the United States until after 1865. The first iron-and-steel-producing foundry on the West Coast was the Pacific Rolling Mill & Forge Company in San Francisco. That company was founded in 1866. Leland Stanford (one of the Central Pacific Railroad's founders) was a large stockholder in the Pacific Rolling Mill & Forge Company. The Central Pacific Railroad issued a contract with Pacific Rolling Mill & Forge Company by 1875 to produce replacement iron rails.

In the 1850s, the citizens of Placer County wanted a railroad connection to the Sacramento Valley Railroad, which ran from Sacramento to Folsom. Theodore Judah wanted to find a railroad route over the Sierras. These two goals were combined into the development of the five-foot-gauge

Sacramento, Placer & Nevada Railroad, which was proposed to run from Folsom through Auburn to the town of Nevada (City). Originally surveyed by Judah and later by Sherman Day, the route proposed for the Sacramento, Placer & Nevada Railroad basically paralleled the present-day Auburn-Folsom Road. The Folsom end had a connection with the California Central Railroad at a spot called Ashland Station (essentially the corner of Greenback Lane and Auburn-Folsom Road). The Sacramento, Placer & Nevada Railroad owned no rolling stock of its own. Instead, Sacramento Valley Railroad trains continued up the new line from Folsom to Auburn Station, a little east of Loomis.

Construction on the Sacramento, Placer & Nevada Railroad began early in 1862, and the road was open for business later that same year. However, it had only extended as far north as Auburn Station, about six miles south of Auburn itself. That location is near the present-day corner of Auburn-Folsom Road and Whisky Bar Road in Loomis. Unfortunately, the construction of the Central Pacific Railroad through nearby Newcastle and into Auburn drew most of the area's rail traffic, causing the Sacramento, Placer & Nevada Railroad to declare bankruptcy. The rails of the Sacramento, Placer & Nevada Railroad were disputed by the Central Pacific and a Sacramento Valley Railroad subsidiary, the Placerville & Sacramento Valley Railroad, in what came to be called the Placer County Railroad Wars. The Placerville & Sacramento Valley Railroad prevailed in the dispute and pulled up the tracks in 1864.

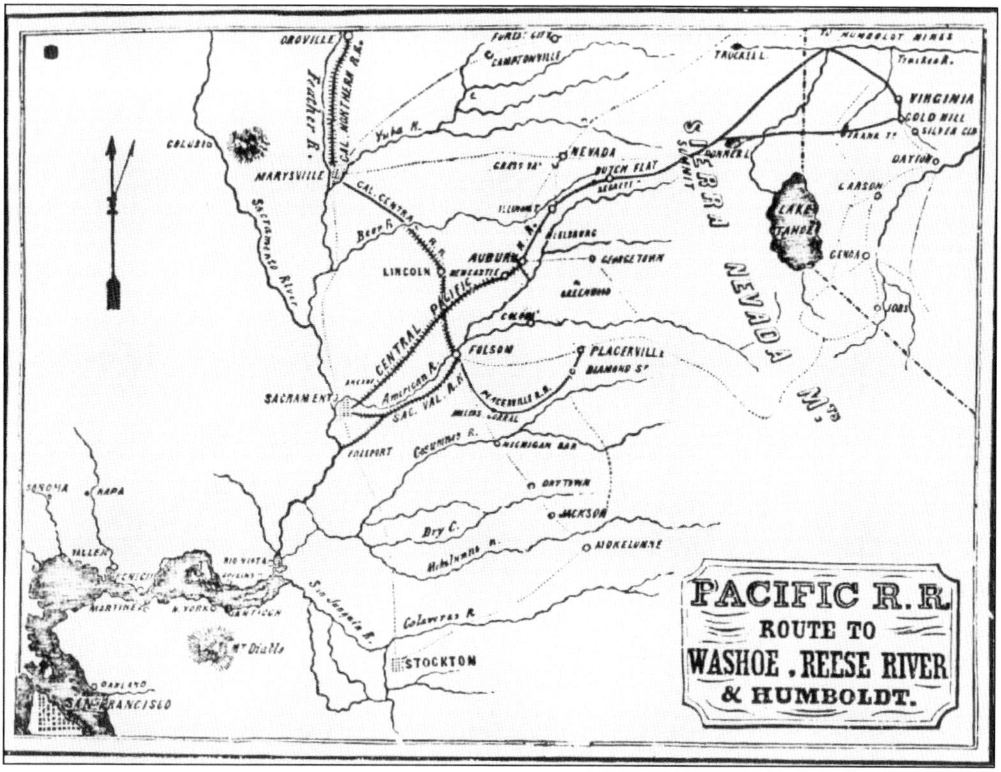

This July 1864 map shows the route for the early railroads in Northern California. The rails that have already been laid are indicated by crosshatches, while the rails that are to be laid in the future are indicated by a simple line. (AJS.)

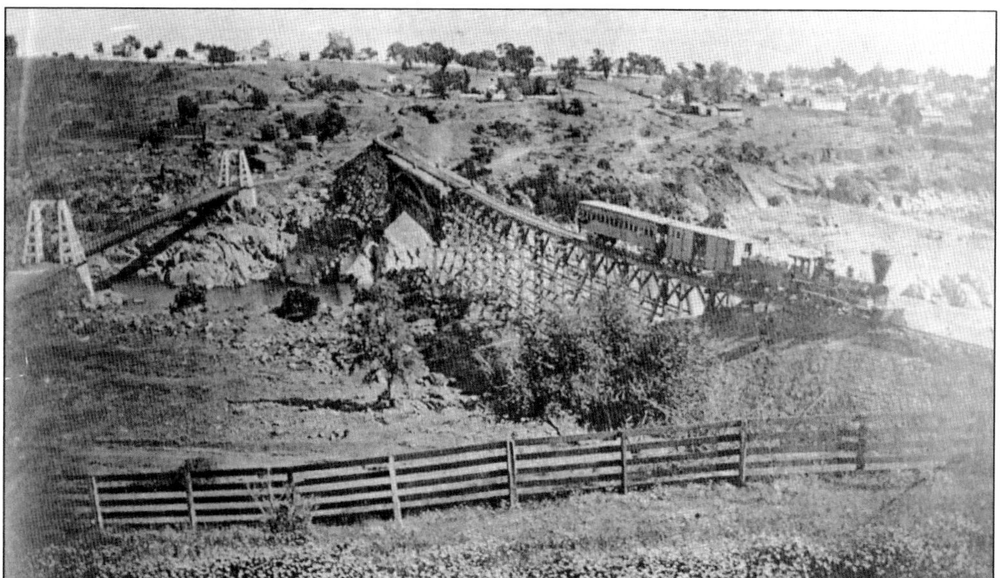

A California Central train leaves Folsom and crosses the railroad company's bridge across the American River. This 1860s-era photograph of the crossing was taken near where the Folsom automobile bridge crosses the American River today. (California State Library.)

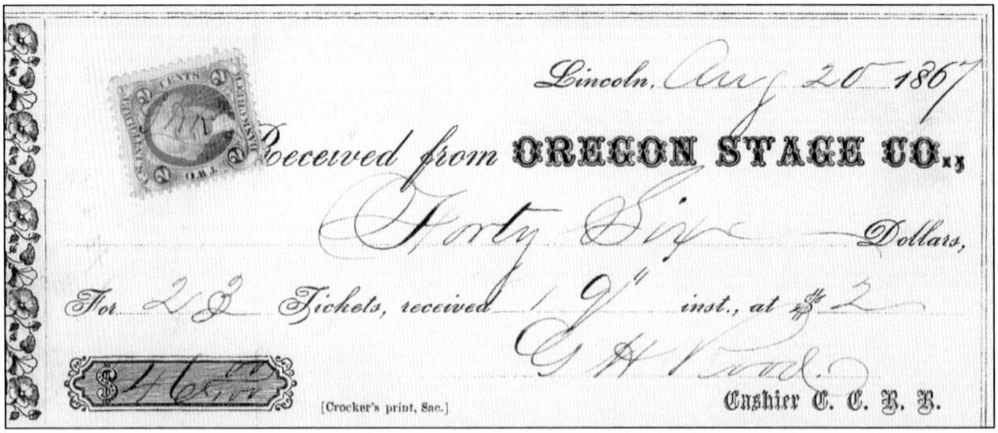
Lincoln, Aug 20 1867

Received from OREGON STAGE CO.,

Forty Six Dollars,

For 22 Tickets, received 19" inst., at $2

$46 00/100

[Crocker's print, Sac.]

Cashier C. C. R. R.

A warrant is a document that certifies or guarantees something such as a receipt for goods stored in a warehouse. *Warrant* is also a 19th-century term for a check. One is shown above with the name of the California Central Railroad's cashier in the lower right corner. The warrant has Lincoln, the northern terminus of the California Central's route, printed on the upper right corner. The Oregon Stage Company was owned by Henry W. Corbett of Portland, Oregon, and ran between Portland and Sacramento, California. It controlled the stagecoach business between California and Oregon until the two states were linked by rail in 1887. (AJS.)

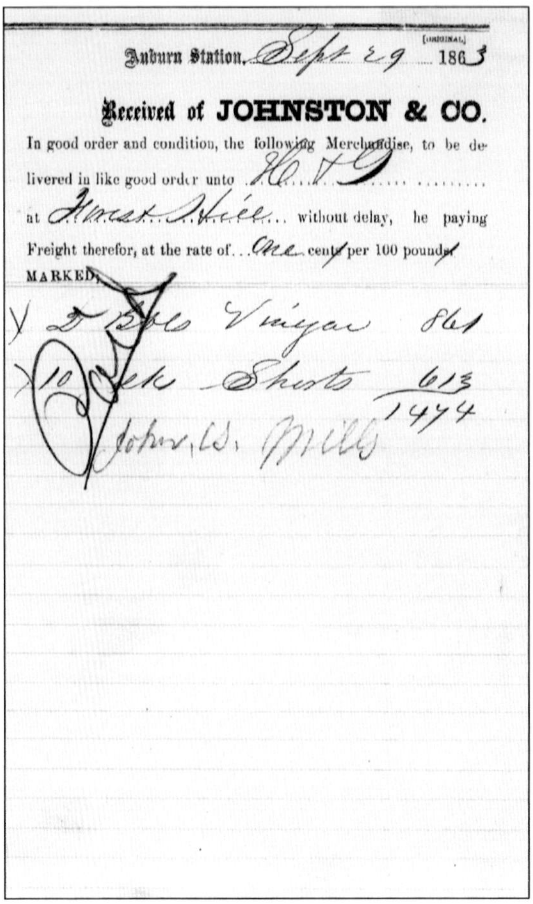
[ORIGINAL]

Auburn Station, Sept 29 1863

Received of JOHNSTON & CO.

In good order and condition, the following Merchandise, to be delivered in like good order unto H & G at Forest Hill without delay, he paying Freight therefor, at the rate of One cents per 100 pounds

MARKED

2 Bbls Vinegar 861

10 Sck Shorts 613

1474

The date 1863 appears on this receipt from Auburn Station, meaning that this is the Auburn Station of the Sacramento, Placer & Nevada Railroad and not the Auburn Station of the Central Pacific Railroad. The Central Pacific did not reach Auburn until 1865. Though the stop was called "Auburn Station," it was actually about six miles south of the town of Auburn, much closer to the town of Loomis. The expectation was that the Sacramento, Placer & Nevada Railroad would extend its line to Auburn and beyond, but Auburn Station was as far north as it got before it declared bankruptcy. (AJS.)

Two

Central Pacific Railroad

Theodore Judah had been chief engineer for two early California railroads—the Sacramento Valley Railroad, running from Sacramento to Folsom, and the Sacramento, Placer & Nevada Railroad, which extended the Folsom line into Placer County toward Auburn. But Judah had bigger dreams. He imagined a transcontinental railroad that would connect California to the rest of the United States.

Judah was a tireless promoter of his idea, but he also put his know-how to work, surveying several possible routes for his proposed railroad to cross the Sierra Nevada. His favored route followed the ridge between the American and Bear Rivers, passing through Placer and Nevada Counties. The nearly uninterrupted ridge greatly reduced the need for time-consuming construction of expensive wooden trestles and bridges and maintained a constant uphill grade to the summit.

In Sacramento, Judah's preliminary plans helped convince a group of local merchants to support his railroad concept, with 30 initially signing on as investors. The principal players were Judah, Collis Huntington, Mark Hopkins, Leland Stanford, Charles Crocker, and James Bailey. Meanwhile, Judah's persistent lobbying in Washington, DC, helped convince the federal government to issue loan bonds to finance the construction of the first transcontinental railroad.

In 1861, the Central Pacific Railroad (CPRR) was incorporated in California, with Theodore Judah as chief engineer. The following year, President Lincoln signed the Pacific Railroad Act, specifying that the Union Pacific would build west from Omaha, Nebraska, while the Central Pacific would build east from Sacramento. As the competing companies completed sections of the new railroad, they received land grants along their surveyed rights-of-way to help pay for the cost of constructing the line.

Ground was broken in Sacramento in January 1863, but actual construction of the line did not begin until that fall. Judah became disenchanted with the priorities of the Central Pacific leaders, and in the fall of 1863, he set out for the East, reportedly to meet with potential new investors. He became ill while crossing Panama and died on November 2 before seeing his dream come true. After Judah's death, Samuel Montague became the Central Pacific's acting chief engineer. By February 1864, the roadbed entered Placer County, crossing Dry Creek 17 miles from Sacramento. In April, trains began running to Junction, where they intersected the Folsom-to-Lincoln line of the California Central. Junction would soon become known as Roseville.

At Rocklin, a yard and roundhouse were built to house equipment and workers for the climb farther into the mountains. Tracks reached Newcastle in June 1864. Beyond Newcastle, the first major construction obstacles were reached. A high, curved trestle was needed east of Newcastle, and at Bloomer Cut, a concrete-like rocky ridge required blasting powder to carve a roadbed through it. In 1865, the railroad pushed farther into Placer County, reaching Auburn in May and Clipper Gap in June before reaching a site near Illinoistown in September 1865, where the new town of Colfax had been laid out on railroad-owned land. Many Chinese were added to the CPRR workforce during 1865, but their fame was yet to come for their accomplishments at Cape Horn and in the mountains beyond.

Over the winter of 1865–1866, major wood trestles were built above Colfax at Long Ravine and Secret Town, and a roadbed was cut into the steep hillside at Cape Horn. The wooden trestles were later filled in with dirt and rocks, a very labor-intensive effort. Still the railroad forged ahead, past the mining towns at Gold Run and Dutch Flat, on to Blue Canyon and Emigrant Gap, then to Cisco, where construction was halted by the harsh winter of 1866. Meanwhile, at Donner Summit, work crews, including Chinese, began the painstaking process of drilling the 1,659-foot-long summit tunnel through solid granite. Although tunnel work continued through the harsh winter, the summit tunnel would not be completed until late in 1867. Grading and track work had to be halted on the mountain during the winter, so three locomotives, track for 40 miles of road, and 40 cars were transported on sleds and wagons from Cisco over the summit to the area then known as Coburn's Station, soon to become Truckee. Crews continued track construction near Coburn's Station until weather allowed renewed grading and track-laying near the summit.

Beyond Emigrant Gap, the new railroad line skirted back and forth over the Placer County–Nevada County line before returning to Placer County for the downhill run from Donner Summit. When the tracks reached Coburn's Station, the rail line was back in Nevada County. Trains began running from Sacramento to Coburn's/Truckee in May 1868. The name change to Truckee became permanent in August 1868, after a fire destroyed Coburn's Station. In May 1869, the Union Pacific and Central Pacific met at Promontory, Utah, thus completing the nation's first transcontinental railroad.

The Central Pacific leaders were not done with railroad construction. In 1869, they bought the fledgling Southern Pacific Railroad, which had begun building south from San Francisco. In 1870, the Southern Pacific and the Central Pacific were combined operationally. In 1885, the two companies were officially merged under a holding company called the Southern Pacific Company. The Central Pacific continued to own the line over Donner Pass, but its rails and equipment were leased to Southern Pacific. By 1901, operations throughout the state were mostly identified under the Southern Pacific name.

The Central Pacific also played a role in another part of Placer County. In 1870, the Central Pacific absorbed the California & Oregon Railroad, which operated the line that ran north from Roseville through Lincoln in Placer County toward Marysville. This later became part of Southern Pacific's Shasta Route to Oregon.

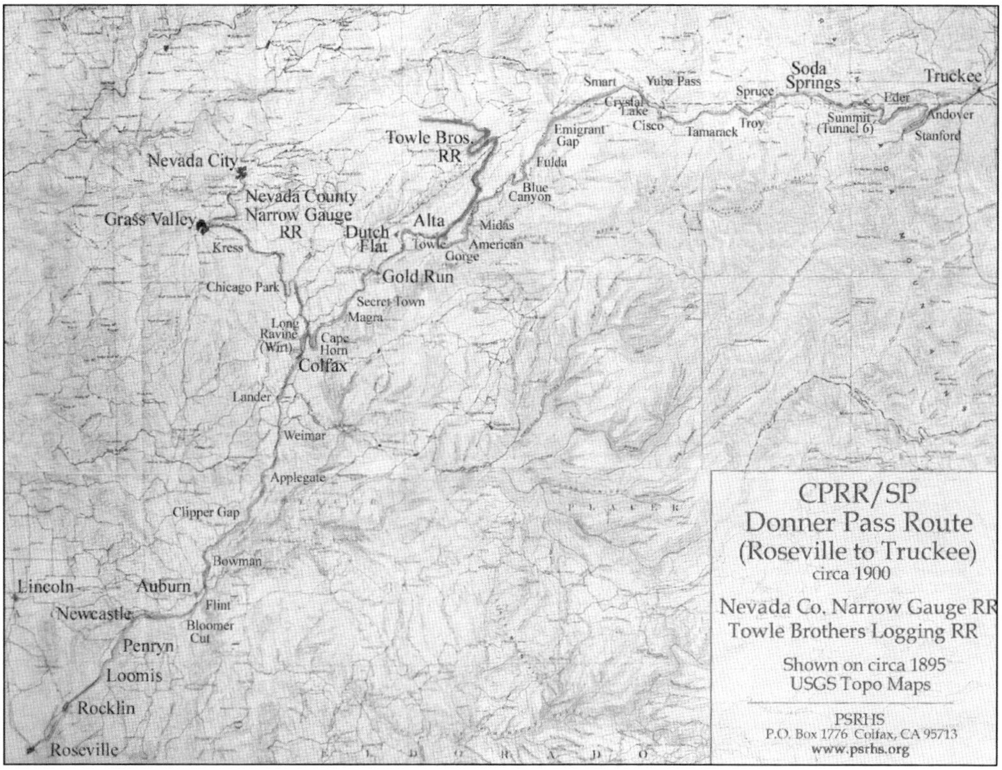

This map shows the route followed by Central Pacific Railroad construction from Roseville to Truckee, with most of this portion of the route within Placer County. Names for many of the early stations or features along the railroad are shown, along with the pre-1900 routes of the Nevada County Narrow Gauge Railroad (see chapter 6) and Towle Brothers' logging railroad (see chapter 7). Construction of the very difficult mountain portion of the original transcontinental railroad was completed from 1864 to 1868. The rail line at lower left, going north from Roseville to Lincoln and beyond, became part of the Central Pacific in 1870. (PSRHS.)

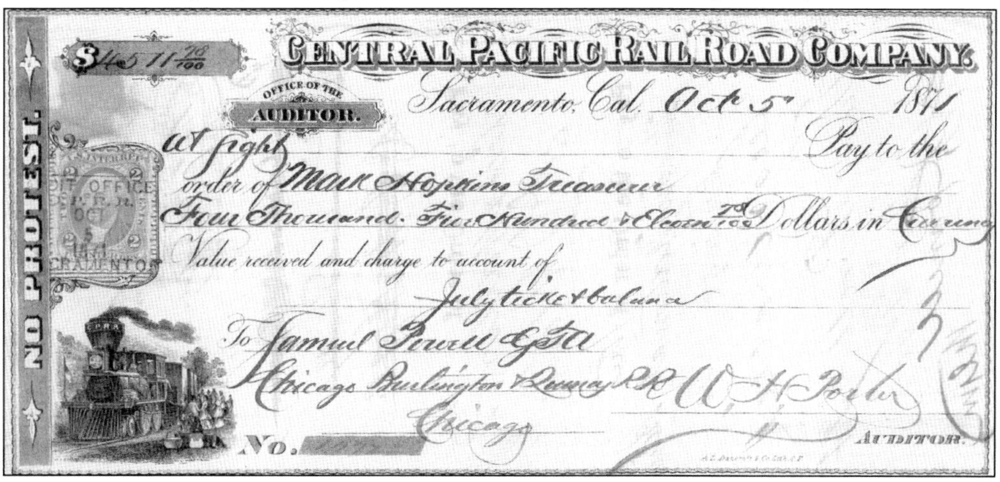

This is an 1871 Central Pacific check that transferred funds between the Central Pacific and Chicago, Burlington & Quincy (CB&Q) Railroad for joint ticket sales on their combined route. Note the details in the CPRR letterhead, images, and revenue stamp on the check. (AJS.)

The *Governor Stanford* was the first locomotive received by the Central Pacific, arriving at Sacramento in September 1863. It was an American-style with four driver wheels and initially provided power to construction trains for building the tracks east from Sacramento. As with all early locomotives purchased by CPRR, this engine came in pieces from the East Coast to Sacramento on board a ship that traveled around the tip of South America. (Alfred Hart/Stanford.)

In early 1864, the Central Pacific tracks entered Placer County, crossing Dry Creek on this wooden bridge. This location is now part of the large Roseville railyard. About a mile farther east, the Central Pacific reached Junction in February 1864. (Junction would soon be renamed Roseville.) At Junction, the Central Pacific crossed the tracks of the California Central Railroad, which ran from Folsom to Lincoln. The California Central would become part of the Central Pacific in 1870. (Alfred Hart/Stanford.)

By March 1864, the Central Pacific tracks had reached the base of the Sierra foothills, from which further construction would be in mountainous, steep terrain. Rocklin was chosen by the CPRR as the location for a station and yard that would serve the railroad's needs during further construction and later operation over Donner Summit. This photograph shows the Rocklin Depot after it was rebuilt following an 1891 fire. (AJS.)

A roundhouse was built at Rocklin to service helper engines that would assist trains making the climb up the mountain. The roundhouse was built with local Rocklin granite. After the railroad arrived, Rocklin granite could be more easily transported to Sacramento and the Bay Area. The granite was used in construction of many major buildings, including the San Francisco Mint. (AJS.)

Another early business opportunity for the railroad was the transportation of Griffith granite quarried at Penryn. This photograph shows the depot at Penryn. A spur track connected the quarry with the railroad line. (AJS.)

Tracks reached Newcastle in June 1864, and scheduled service started between Sacramento and Newcastle on June 6. A temporary turntable was set up at Newcastle to turn locomotives for the return trip. Note construction of the roadbed behind the turntable and the curved trestle extending into the distance. (Alfred Hart/Ken Yeo.)

The tracks were halted at Newcastle while the curved trestle seen in the previous image was built to traverse a ravine that interrupted the ridgeline. In the photograph above, the trestle is shown only partially constructed. The photograph below shows the completed trestle with a train crossing over it. These early structures did safely support the trains, but it must have taken a leap of faith for the engineers to drive their locomotives across them. This trestle was later filled in. (Above, Alfred Hart/Ken Yeo; below, Alfred Hart/Stanford.)

Beyond Newcastle, the next major obstacle encountered was a ridge of very dense, cemented volcanic mudflow that resembled concrete. Cutting a path for the railroad through this material required the use of blasting powder. The resulting cut is known as Bloomer Cut and exists today just west of Auburn much as it looked after being initially cut in 1865. The photograph above shows tracks approaching the cut from the west. Below, a train passes through the cut. (Both, Alfred Hart/Ken Yeo.)

The tracks reached Auburn in May 1865. This scene shows an early view of the Auburn depot area. One of the buildings was the freight depot. The other housed an eating house and saloon; it was soon replaced with a two-story structure operated by Thomas Curley and James Mahon. During the early construction, the Central Pacific made deals with local businesspeople to build and operate an eating house on railroad land if they also provided space for railroad ticket sales. (Alfred Hart/Stanford.)

A small depot existed at Applegate east of Auburn. Even the smallest communities had depots. Baggage is being loaded onto an eastbound train that has stopped at Applegate. The depot building is at the right edge of the image. This location is now adjacent to the Interstate 80 eastbound off-ramp at Applegate. (AJS.)

The new town of Colfax was laid out in July 1865 on land owned by the Central Pacific. The railroad arrived in September, bypassing nearby Illinoistown by a couple of miles. This scene shows a train approaching Colfax from the west. The large piles of wood by the tracks are fuel for the locomotives. (AJS.)

The building to the right side of the tracks is the original Colfax passenger depot, and the long building at left is the freight shed. Colfax became a major freight distribution point for nearby communities and mines and supported construction of the railroad further into the mountains. The CPRR tracks ended at Colfax until the spring of 1866. (Alfred Hart/Stanford.)

This close-up view shows a Central Pacific train with two locomotives stopped beside the freight shed. The lead locomotive is No. 68, the *Peoquop*, a 10-wheeler with six driving wheels built in 1868. Note the piles of firewood in the tenders behind the locomotives and the nearly barren hillsides beyond the freight shed. (Ken Yeo.)

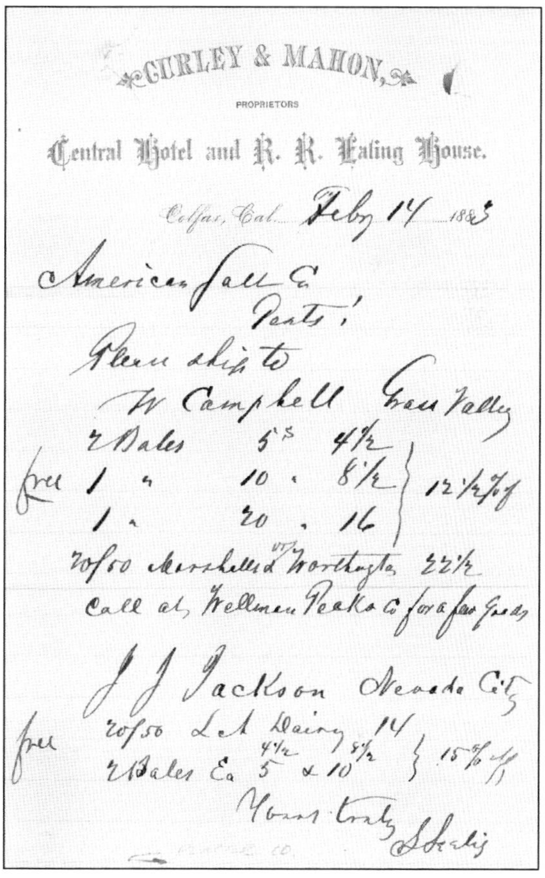

CURLEY & MAHON,
PROPRIETORS
Central Hotel and R. R. Eating House.
Colfax, Cal. Feby 14 1883

American Salt Co
Parts;
Please ship to
W Campbell Grass Valley
2 Bales 5s 4½
free 1 " 10 " 8½ } 12½% of
1 " 20 " 16
20/50 Marshall & Worthington 22½
Call at Wellman Peake & Co for a few goods

J J Jackson Nevada City
free 20/50 Lot Dairy 14
2 Bales Ea 5 & 10 4½ 8½ } 15% off
Yours truly

The eating house in the Colfax passenger depot was operated by Thomas Curley and James Mahon. They also operated the nearby Central Hotel. The quality of the food at the eating house was well known among travelers. In the Central Pacific's early days, meal stops were scheduled at certain locations along the line. The eating houses were judged by both the quality of the food and the speed of service. The 1883 note at right displays the letterhead for Curley and Mahon's Colfax eating house and hotel. (AJS.)

Just east of Colfax, a large wooden trestle and a wooden bridge were built to traverse two dips in the terrain at Long Ravine. This photograph shows the bridge portion with a Central Pacific train crossing over it. Later, the Nevada County Narrow Gauge Railroad tracks passed under this bridge. The trestle portion is to the left of the bridge in this view. (Alfred Hart/Stanford.)

The Long Ravine Bridge traverses the nearest branch of the ravine in this view, while the curved trestle crosses the second part near the center of the image. By 1876, the curved trestle had been filled in, but the bridge remained. The town of Colfax is just beyond the left edge of the image. (AJS.)

A track-level perspective looking westbound shows the Long Ravine Bridge in the foreground and the curved Long Ravine Trestle in the distance. Note that the bridge sides and piers have been covered to reduce the effects of the weather and prolong their life. (AJS.)

This later view shows a Central Pacific train on the Long Ravine Bridge and a better view of the bridge itself. Note the man on top of the train and another standing on the bridge. The curved wooden trestle is no longer visible beyond the bridge—the trestle was covered with fill material by 1876, as were most of the wooden trestles built along the route. (PSRHS.)

Beyond Long Ravine, the railroad faced a different problem. The roadbed had to be carved out of the steep hillside at Cape Horn. This photograph shows a locomotive rounding Cape Horn on tracks cut into the steep hillside. While the stories of Chinese workers suspended in baskets for this work have been disproved, creating the roadbed around Cape Horn was a major achievement. (Alfred Hart/Stanford.)

This image from a stereograph shows the sharp drop from Cape Horn into the canyon below the tracks and the North Fork of the American River far below. For several years, trains stopped here to let passengers take in the view. Note the wooden bridge crossing the river in the distance that linked Colfax with Iowa Hill. (AJS.)

In this classic view at Secret Town, an impressive wooden trestle was built to cross a low area, and work is already under way to fill it in. A multitude of Chinese workers are using handcarts to slowly and methodically cover the trestle with fill material. Today, the curved fill is briefly visible from Interstate 80, which cuts diagonally across the area to the right of the tracks. (PSRHS.)

At Dutch Flat, the tracks passed by on the hillside above the town. A building next to the tracks housed a saloon and boardinghouse operated by the Faller family. It also served as the Dutch Flat Depot and figured prominently in the railroad accident shown on the next page. (AJS.)

Dutch Flat was the scene of a major railroad accident in 1898 when the boiler of a train's lead locomotive exploded while passing the station. The photograph above shows the damage done to the locomotive. Its mangled cab was tossed a considerable distance by the explosion. The engineer and fireman were both killed by the blast, along with an unidentified third person. The loss of life could have been worse. The photograph below shows damage to the nearby Faller boardinghouse. Four people, including three members of the Faller family, were injured by flying debris. The locomotive had just taken on water at the previous stop and the boiler was full, so the cause of the explosion was a mystery. (Both, Ken Yeo.)

In the 1870s, Placer County lumberman Alan Towle and his brothers expanded their logging operations at a siding on the Central Pacific a mile above Alta. Their railroad and related businesses are described in chapter 7. They established a company town called Towle that included the Kearsarge Hotel at right and general store at left. Today, nothing remains of this once-bustling company town. (AJS.)

Beyond Towle, the railroad tracks returned to the edge of the canyon for several miles. This scene shows a stop at a location called American that featured a concrete platform and broad vistas looking down into the canyon of the North Fork of the American River. (AJS.)

At an elevation of 4,695 feet, Blue Canyon (spelled Canon in early references) experienced heavy winter snows. Snowsheds were soon erected from here to the summit and beyond to protect the tracks from the drifting snow. The small community looks comfortable in this summer photograph, but two trains were stalled near here for nearly two weeks in the blizzard of 1890. The start of the snowsheds can be seen beyond the buildings. (AJS.)

Where ample fill material was available nearby, construction crews would sometimes fill a gap directly rather than building a trestle and filling it in later. This is shown in progress at Heath's Ravine east of Blue Canyon using material from a cut in the distance. (Alfred Hart/Stanford.)

Emigrant Gap was named for the gap in the ridge between the North Fork of the American River and the Bear River, through which early emigrant wagon trains passed on their way to the Sacramento valley. This view shows a train stopped on the tracks near Emigrant Gap. (AJS.)

Snowsheds were eventually built to cover nearly the entire distance from Blue Canyon to the summit and part of the way down the eastern slope. Fire was a constant danger from sparks generated by the locomotives and the dry wood of the sheds. An extensive section of the sheds seen here at Emigrant Gap was destroyed by a costly fire in 1901, but portions were rebuilt. (AJS.)

Tracks reached Cisco in the fall of 1866, but snowfall that winter was so heavy that the line could not be kept open, and operations retreated to Alta. This view of snow at Cisco shows why management decided in favor of the costly but necessary construction of snowsheds. (PSRHS.)

This view of snowsheds at Cisco shows just a small portion of the over 30 miles of sheds that were built to protect the tracks from winter's blast. Many of the sheds did not have openings along their length, creating a dark, smoky environment for train crews and passengers and leading to the label "railroading in a barn." (AJS.)

Summit Station, adjacent to Summit Tunnel 6, was built entirely within snowsheds. The sheds covered not only the tracks curving in the foreground but also the engine shed at right and the turntable at the center. Some sheds had vents in the roof to release smoke generated by the locomotives. The hotel and other buildings were connected to the sheds by covered walkways. (California State Library.)

This photograph shows the inside of a snowshed. Wind-blown snow filtered into the sheds through small cracks. Note the station at right, located inside the shed, and the woman climbing the ladder to hang orders for the train crew. (AJS.)

Tunnels near the summit had to be chiseled and blasted out of solid granite. This view shows a Chinese water or tea bearer near the east portal of Tunnel 8. Chinese workers brought their culture with them, working in teams with their own cook. Their preference for tea made with boiling water is cited as a reason the Chinese had fewer illnesses than other workers. (Alfred Hart/Stanford.)

This view looking into Tunnel 12 illustrates the major effort it took to carve a tunnel out of solid rock without benefit of modern tools. Internal bracing that was sometimes needed can be seen in the depths of this tunnel. (AJS.)

Snow removal from the tracks was an issue before snowsheds were built and was still needed in some areas not protected by sheds or where sheds had burned. This photograph shows one of the early bucker plows used by the Central Pacific. Several engines would ram the plow into a bank of snow, back up to get another run at it, and surge forward again. (AJS.)

Bucker plows derailed often and had difficulty pushing the heavy snow from the tracks. Rotary plows offered a way to throw the snow out of the way rather than merely pushing it. This photograph shows an early rotary called a cyclone. It looked promising, but its corkscrew design performed poorly in Sierra snow and was not pursued. (AJS.)

This style of rotary plow with its spinning wheel and ability to throw snow in either direction played an essential role in clearing the tracks during the blizzard of 1890. It became the prototype for future rotaries purchased and used by the Central Pacific. (PSRHS.)

This photograph shows the railroad tracks dropping down the eastern slope of the snowy Sierra Nevada near Donner Lake. The snowshed-covered tracks can be seen snaking down the mountainside to the right. The tracks are in Placer County, while the lake is in Nevada County. (AJS.)

Three

Southern Pacific Railroad

As parent company to the Central Pacific after 1885, Southern Pacific (SP) assumed more and more operational control over the Central Pacific railroad routes through Placer and Nevada Counties. With numerous railroad lines now under its control, Southern Pacific began a systematic renumbering of locomotives in the 1890s to minimize confusion and duplication of identifying numbers. By 1901, most locomotives, rolling stock, and buildings displayed the Southern Pacific name. A new and larger yard was opened in Roseville in 1906, replacing the yard and roundhouse in Rocklin. Meanwhile, increasing business along the transcontinental route over Donner Pass began to create congestion on the single track shared by both eastbound and westbound trains. Southern Pacific decided a second track was needed to reduce congestion and the risk of head-on collisions.

From 1909 to 1915, a second track was built from Rocklin to Colfax. The new track followed a slightly longer route to reduce the grade for uphill trains. The old track was modified at Rocklin to go under the new track, while the new track went under the old track near Applegate. At times, the two tracks came close together but at different elevations, creating challenges for the construction crews, because freight and passenger trains had to continue running during the construction. The original track remained largely unchanged, but some of the curves were eliminated by using newer construction equipment, and small sections of the original roadbed were abandoned. At Colfax, hillsides were cut away to straighten the track through town, and a large yard and an enginehouse were built. Helper engines were stationed at Colfax to be added to trains going over Donner Pass. A wye track was also added for turning engines, replacing a turntable that had been in use for 10 years. To turn an engine using a wye track, the engine was driven off the main track onto one branch of the wye to its base, then backed out on the other branch, returning it to the main track but facing in the opposite direction.

In 1915, construction of the second track continued above Colfax to Blue Canyon, adding a second bridge at Long Ravine. Most of the new track on this portion of the route was laid alongside the original line, but at Cape Horn, two new double-track tunnels were drilled to bypass the original route around "the Cape." The curves in these tunnels soon proved to be too tight for long locomotives and cars to pass each other safely, and the tunnels were single-tracked, with the uphill trains moved back to the original tracks around Cape Horn. After a delay to resolve legal disputes between the government and Southern Pacific, double-track work above Blue Canyon resumed in the early 1920s. A new facility was built at Norden from 1924 to 1925 that included a large turntable to turn helper locomotives, a cookhouse, and crew facilities—all located inside snowsheds or connected by covered tunnels because of the heavy snowfall the area receives. Beyond Norden, a new 10,320-foot-long Summit Tunnel 41 was completed for the second track in 1925. East of the tunnel, the two tracks converged and ran side by side to Truckee.

Southern Pacific began to introduce bigger locomotives to haul the increasing freight loads over the mountains. To support these heavier locomotives, SP began replacing the lighter-weight rails in 1902 with 90-pound steel rails. The larger locomotives also created another issue: crews experienced problems from the smoke and fumes that built up when steaming through the tunnels and extensive snowsheds. This led to development of cab-forward locomotives. The cab-forward design became the workhorse of the route over Donner Pass and one of SP's signature locomotives until the late 1940s, when diesel power began replacing steam.

SP operated numerous premier passenger trains that connected with Union Pacific trains in Ogden, Utah. Passenger traffic increased considerably during World War II, but after the war, the popularity of automobiles and better highways began to reduce rail passenger travel. In the 1950s and 1960s, SP began to favor freight loads over passenger trains. In 1971, Amtrak took over most of the nation's passenger trains and preserved passenger service over Donner Pass. Roseville and Truckee were early Amtrak stops. In 1976, Amtrak added passenger service at Colfax. After 2000, Capitol Corridor trains brought passenger service back to Auburn and Rocklin.

By 1994, SP was beginning to lose freight business on the Donner Route to rail and highway competitors. Management made the decision to eliminate some of the double track over Donner Summit and move the rail to other, more lucrative parts of the SP system. Although upgraded through the years, most of the original transcontinental route built by Central Pacific over Donner Summit was still in use. But in 1994, the railroad tracks were torn up along the original line from Norden through the series of tunnels at the summit built in the 1860s, hand-carved by laborers into the granite peaks. Today, all trains cross over Donner Summit through the newer Tunnel 41.

In the late 1800s and through most of the 1900s, the Southern Pacific Company grew to be a major Class I railroad system. Along with the Donner Route through Placer County from Sacramento to Ogden, SP provided service north to Portland and to northwestern California, south to Los Angeles by both the Coast and San Joaquin Routes, east from Los Angeles on the southern route to Tucson, El Paso, and New Orleans, and into Mexico. A planned merger with Santa Fe Railway in 1983 failed to get federal approval. In 1988, management of SP was absorbed by the company that controlled the Denver & Rio Grande Western Railroad. Southern Pacific ended its impressive run in 1996 when it became part of the Union Pacific Railroad. The SP name and logo soon began to disappear from view in Placer County, replaced by Union Pacific colors and markings.

The Central Pacific name was still appearing in Placer County in the 1890s, although the line had been leased to Southern Pacific in 1885. Central Pacific Locomotive No. 2000 was built in 1892 and put in service that year. It appeared in Sacramento in 1893 with the same Central Pacific markings. This locomotive became SP No. 2847 in 1901, then No. 2947 in 1906, marking the shift from the Central Pacific to Southern Pacific names along the route. (AJS.)

The Central Pacific absorbed the California Central line from Folsom to Lincoln in 1870. By 1901, the Southern Pacific name had replaced the Central Pacific in the region. This early-1900s photograph shows the Lincoln Depot in Placer County on SP's Shasta Route. (AJS.)

This January 1905 photograph shows the Rocklin-based crew posed on two steam locomotives in the roundhouse. A year later, the Rocklin Roundhouse was shut down when the yard operations were moved to nearby Roseville. Harry Rasmussen is the teenager sitting in the foreground. Rasmussen later went to work for SP, and in 1952, he missed by a day being assigned as engineer on the *City of San Francisco* that became snowbound near Donner Summit for several days (see page 60). (Andrew Brandon.)

The Rocklin Depot is at far left, the freight building lies beyond the locomotive, and the roundhouse is at far right. Railroad business in Rocklin dropped dramatically when the roundhouse and yard were moved from Rocklin to Roseville in 1906. Note the business buildings beyond the freight building. (AJS.)

With the move of its main yard from Rocklin to Roseville in 1906, SP had room to build a larger yard with two roundhouses, one devoted to helper locomotives for the climb over Donner Pass. This aerial view taken from a kite in 1910 shows a portion of the Roseville yard with the two roundhouses and turntables clearly visible. (AJS.)

This ground-level view shows one of the two roundhouses at Roseville with a cab-forward locomotive on the turntable. See pages 53 and 63 for more information on the cab-forward design. (PSRHS.)

This is another view of the Roseville yard. The Southern Pacific clubhouse is the large building at the far left. The clubhouse provided sleeping quarters, food service, and activities for train crews between runs. (AJS.)

Roseville's yard included a large icing plant where ice was added to early refrigerated boxcars to protect precious cargoes of fruit and other perishables on the journey east. The icing plant became obsolete when mechanical refrigeration was added to the railcars in the late 1950s. (AJS.)

After Roseville became the main yard for SP in Placer County, a new passenger depot was built at the east end of the yard in the triangle formed where the northern Shasta Route connected with the east-west route to Ogden. This postcard image shows the depot building with a locomotive and cars moving past it. (PSRHS.)

This more distant view shows the Roseville Depot and its location relative to the straight-ahead tracks heading towards Donner Pass and Ogden and the curved track turning northward towards Oregon. (AJS.)

From 1909 to 1915, a second track was added between Rocklin and Colfax. Except at a few locations, the original track was untouched, while the new track was often built near it but following a longer route to reduce the rate of climb. This scene shows Newcastle before the second track was added. Here, the original route in the foreground was realigned and a new crossing built over the ravine in the distance. (AJS.)

A new double-track tunnel was built beyond the ravine at Newcastle. Note the original track angling to the left, which was kept operational while the tunnel was being bored. (AJS.)

This unique view was captured from the hillside above the tunnel looking back across the ravine towards Newcastle. Old and new tracks have been shifted to the new fill over the ravine, while the old curving roadbed can be seen to the left of the new grade. Today, Interstate 80 passes under the tracks from left to right at this ravine. (AJS.)

A train derailment at Newcastle resulted in a big cleanup of strewn and damaged railcars. Main line tracks angle to the left, while a portion of the original track alignment is visible curving to the right. (Ken Yeo.)

As the new uphill track (called Track 2) approached Auburn, it crossed Auburn Ravine and the road from Auburn to Newcastle on a high steel trestle. In this 1911 photograph, the trestle construction is reaching out across Auburn Ravine from the Newcastle side on tall steel pylons. The new Track 2 circled Auburn on the northwest, while the original track was on the southeast. (AJS.)

The trestle has extended almost to the Nevada Street side of Auburn Ravine in this photograph taken from the Newcastle side looking toward Auburn. Today, Interstate 80 passes under the trestle. (AJS.)

While the Auburn Ravine Trestle was being built, temporary tracks were laid along Sacramento Street in old Auburn so a special work train including a steam shovel could be moved from the old Track 1 to the construction site along Nevada Street. Once there, the construction of the roadbed and track laying could continue before the trestle was completed. (Dave Ferreira.)

Since the new Track 2 bypassed the east Auburn depot, a station was built on Nevada Street on land now occupied by Echo Valley Ranch Hay & Feed Store. Auburn now had two depots, the Nevada Street depot for eastbound passengers and the Lincoln Street depot for westbound trains. (Ken Yeo.)

Track 1 near the Auburn Depot is being cleared in the aftermath of a derailment. The depot building can be seen in the distance on the left beyond the Auburn Lumber Company yard, formerly a Towle Brothers retail lumberyard. (PSRHS.)

At times during World War II, the Auburn Depot was host to an Army medical train that stopped to transfer patients to the Dewitt Hospital in North Auburn, then a large Army medical facility. Note the POW helper (the man with the large "PW" on his back) at the rear of the nearest ambulance. (Ken Yeo.)

Until well into the 1900s, the railroads were the primary means of shipping all sorts of goods between locations near the lines. The image at right is a bill of lading from 1904 processed at the Southern Pacific depot in Auburn. The item being shipped was a basket of laundry from an Auburn business to a customer at Emigrant Gap. Other shipments from Auburn in 1904 included household goods, hardware, blasting powder, sacks of spuds, cases of eggs, a chicken coop, beer, and soda—just about anything and everything. (PSRHS.)

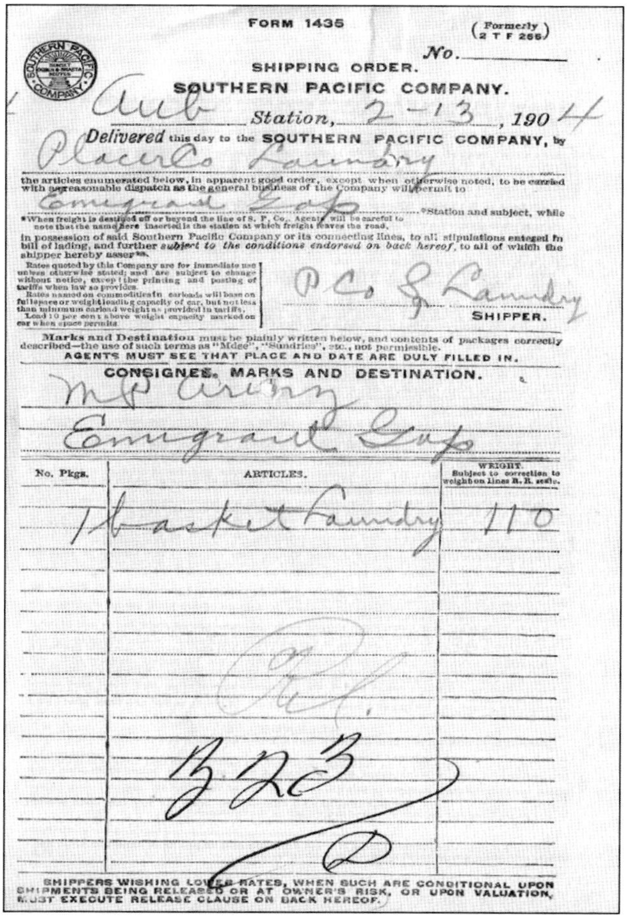

FORM 1435 (Formerly 2 T F 265)

No. ________

SHIPPING ORDER.

SOUTHERN PACIFIC COMPANY.

Aub Station, 2-13, 1904

Delivered this day to the SOUTHERN PACIFIC COMPANY, by Placer Co Laundry

the articles enumerated below, in apparent good order, except when otherwise noted, to be carried with reasonable dispatch as the general business of the Company will permit to Emigrant Gap *Station and subject, while

*When freight is destined off or beyond the line of S. P. Co., Agents will be careful to note that the name here inserted is the station at which freight leaves the road,

in possession of said Southern Pacific Company or its connecting lines, to all stipulations entered in bill of lading, and further *subject to the conditions endorsed on back hereof*, to all of which the shipper hereby assents.

Rates quoted by this Company are for immediate use unless otherwise stated; and are subject to change without notice, except the printing and posting of tariffs when law so provides.

Rates named on commodities in carloads will base on full space or weight loading capacity of car, but not less than minimum carload weight as provided in tariffs.

Load 10 per cent above weight capacity marked on car when space permits.

P Co S Laundry

SHIPPER.

Marks and Destination must be plainly written below, and contents of packages correctly described—the use of such terms as "Mdse", "Sundries", etc., not permissible.

AGENTS MUST SEE THAT PLACE AND DATE ARE DULY FILLED IN.

CONSIGNEE, MARKS AND DESTINATION.

M P Arony

Emigrant Gap

No. Pkgs.	ARTICLES.	WEIGHT. Subject to correction in weigh on lines R. R. scale.
1	basket Laundry	110

323

SHIPPERS WISHING LOWER RATES, WHEN SUCH ARE CONDITIONAL UPON SHIPMENTS BEING RELEASED OR AT OWNER'S RISK, OR UPON VALUATION, MUST EXECUTE RELEASE CLAUSE ON BACK HEREOF.

An old postcard view shows Clipper Gap Depot around 1907, just prior to double tracking. Note the locomotive at far right and the people in the field watching the train pass. (PSRHS.)

Just beyond Clipper Gap above Lake Theodore, the desired path of the longer Track 2 cut across the old line at a sharp curve where the old line rounded a hillside. To avoid this conflict, the hillside in the foreground is being cut back so the original Track 1 can be moved farther south, thus flattening the curve. The new Track 2 will merge with Track 1 on the widened roadbed being created. Ignore the date written in the upper right of the image. (AJS.)

A few miles farther east, the old and new tracks were still close together but at different elevations. It was a challenge to construct the new Track 2 so close to the existing Track 1 but slightly below it and to bore the new Tunnel 23 so close to existing Tunnel 0. A portion of the new tunnel caved in during construction due to its proximity to the existing track. (AJS.)

Between Clipper Gap and Applegate, the new Track 2 crossed under the old Track 1. The photograph above shows the existing track passing diagonally across the view and the underpass being constructed that will allow the new track to go under it. The underpass is complete in the photograph below. This became Tunnel 26. (Both, AJS.)

A serious accident occurred in 1944 when SP's Challenger passenger train went off the tracks at Lander, just west of Colfax. At least nine people were killed in the mangled cars, including four members of the armed services, and more than 100 were injured. The train was carrying numerous military personnel on furlough as well as regular passengers. (Tony Hesch.)

The strange-looking railcar next to the new Colfax Depot (built in 1905) is a McKeen motor car. From 1909 to the early 1930s, these self-propelled, gasoline-powered cars provided local passenger service between Colfax and Sacramento and between Truckee and Reno. (PSRHS.)

As part of the double-tracking project, a new yard was created at Colfax complete with a nine-stall enginehouse and a wye track for turning locomotives. The enginehouse was soon home to a fleet of helper locomotives that assisted eastbound trains on the uphill climb as far as Emigrant Gap. (AJS.)

One of SP's cab-forward locomotives went off the end of the wye track in Colfax when it was being turned. The cab-forward design put the engine crew in front of the smoke and gases produced by the large locomotive that then built up in the tunnels and snowsheds when traversing Donner Summit. (AJS.)

A Colfax-based helper and a cab-forward locomotive are at the front of an eastbound train about to depart Colfax. The Colfax helper would assist as far as Emigrant Gap, where it was cut out or uncoupled, turned on the Emigrant Gap turntable, and returned to Colfax for its next assignment. (PSRHS.)

The circus was in town in this 1937 view of downtown Colfax. A Nevada County Narrow Gauge train is on the right. Beyond the depot and railway express building, circus tents are being set up next to a Southern Pacific train of circus cars. The freight depot is in the distance next to downtown buildings. (PSRHS.)

Prior to double-tracking, a large fill and a single steel bridge, or viaduct, crossed Long Ravine where the Central Pacific wooden trestle and bridge once stood. This photograph shows an eastbound passenger train approaching the steel bridge, which in 1890 replaced the wooden bridge shown on pages 24 and 25. (AJS.)

The aerial view at right shows the railroad tracks at Long Ravine after a second steel bridge, or viaduct, was added in 1915 for the new second track. This 1957 view looks westbound towards Colfax. The construction under way beneath the bridges is for Interstate 80. (AJS.)

Two new double-track tunnels were drilled at Cape Horn with the intent to abandon the tracks around "the Cape." The first tunnel is visible near the sloping hillside in the distance in this view looking at Cape Horn from what is now Highway 174 near Colfax. (PSRHS.)

The tight tunnel curvature did not allow for satisfactory clearance when the large cab-forward locomotives passed each other in the Cape Horn tunnels. The solution was to reactivate the track around Cape Horn for eastbound trains and single-track the tunnels for westbound. Soon, trains were once again rounding Cape Horn. (AJS.)

These photographs show two of the gas-powered vehicles ("putt-putt cars") used by signal maintenance crews to patrol the line and get to trouble spots for repairs. The left image was taken at Cisco. On the right is author Art Sommers's father at Towle. (Both, AJS.)

Several passengers are patiently awaiting the arrival of their train at the Alta Depot. The sign above the door on the right indicates that the post office was once housed in the depot. In this photograph, the depot is located on the south side of the tracks, but it was later moved to the north side. (AJS.)

Snowsheds were built starting at Blue Canyon to combat the heavy snowfall there and farther up the mountain. This scene shows part of the community and the depot in the foreground under winter's snowy blanket. The wooden snowsheds once continued to the summit and beyond. (AJS.)

Fulda Depot was located three miles west of Emigrant Gap. In the early 1900s, the Fulda siding was a busy location for picking up carloads of lumber from nearby logging operations. SP later built a balloon track near Fulda, a large reversing loop that eliminated the need for the turntable at Emigrant Gap. (Herman Darr.)

The photograph above shows the early road that crossed the railroad tracks above Emigrant Gap at grade. But grade crossings are dangerous, and when Highway 40 was rebuilt, the crossing was modified as shown below, sending the highway under the tracks. When Interstate 80 was built, the new freeway crossed above the tracks. (Both, AJS.)

In 1952, the westbound *City of San Francisco* was approaching Yuba Gap in a heavy snowstorm when it ran into a snowslide and became stuck. The train was nearly covered by the drifting snow. Rescue teams brought supplies from Emigrant Gap by foot and snowcat as the passengers had to remain with the train. Other crews worked to clear nearby Highway 40 of avalanches, and the road was finally opened to a spot below the train. After three days of being snowbound, passengers were taken by automobiles to Emigrant Gap, where they boarded another train to complete their journey. The Donner Route remained shut down to normal train traffic for 10 more days. (Both, Ken Yeo.)

At Norden, a new facility was built as part of SP's double-tracking effort. This facility was completely covered in snowsheds, including a 120-foot turntable. These two photographs show construction of the facility and turntable in 1924. A cab-forward is being turned in the above image. The new snowsheds were made of concrete instead of wood and were assembled from prefabricated posts and sections manufactured in Colfax and erected on-site. Portions of the old wooden sheds were retained as part of the new facility. (Both, Ken Yeo.)

There was still a danger of fire in the miles of wooden snowsheds that remained. A fire train was kept at the ready in its own shed at Norden. Locomotive No. 2252 is now on display in Roseville. (Ken Yeo.)

Newer snow-removal equipment reduced the need for some portions of the costly snowsheds. Where sheds were still needed, they were gradually replaced with concrete sheds to reduce the fire danger and maintenance costs. Some light filtered into the sheds through small openings, but inside still had a dark, tunnellike appearance. (PSRHS.)

Whether inside wooden or concrete sheds, the steam locomotives produced a dangerous build-up of smoke and gases. This photograph of a cab-forward emerging from Tunnel 8 ahead of the billowing cloud of smoke clearly illustrates why the cab-forward design was favored by train crews. (Ken Yeo.)

Tunnels also required refurbishing as years passed. When tunnels along the route over Donner Summit were increased in height to allow for newer cars hauling bigger loads, Tunnel 7 was daylighted before it received a new concrete cover. This photograph shows later-model diesels exiting Tunnel 7 towards Tunnel 6. (PSRHS.)

Jordan spreaders are used to plow accumulating snow away from the tracks. This early open-air spreader had no cab to protect the crew from the elements. The wings could be hydraulically adjusted to the desired width for snow clearing. The railcar behind the locomotive is a flanger that cleared snow from between the rails. (AJS.)

Since the 1890 blizzard, rotary plows have been the last line of defense in keeping tracks over Donner Pass open during heavy winter storms. Rotaries can throw the snow a great distance from the tracks in either direction. This rotary and its crew pose at Blue Canyon around 1914. Similar rotaries are still in use today. (AJS.)

Four

Sacramento Northern Railway

The Sacramento Northern Railway, an over-180-mile-long electric-powered interurban railway, connected the city of Chico in the northern part of California's Central Valley with San Francisco in the Bay Area. A central hub for the entire railway system was the capital city of Sacramento. Electric-powered cars could run directly on the streets of Oakland, Sacramento, Yuba City, Chico, and Woodland. The Sacramento Northern Railway ran passenger service until 1941 and freight service into the 1960s. The Sacramento Northern was an important and vital means of transportation until World War II, but the growing use of automobiles, along with competing diesel-powered railroads such as Southern Pacific, were contributing factors to the demise of this interurban line.

What stood out about this railway company was the unique combination of equipment over which its cars and electric freight trains operated. Between the main terminals at Chico and San Francisco, a passenger making the 180-plus-mile trip would encounter the following: third-rail power between Chico and Sacramento, with trolley pole operation through the cities; overhead wire power south of Sacramento, with power pickup by trolley pole and pantograph systems (a mechanical linkage that can be seen at the top of page 71); an interurban car ferry trip across Suisun Bay; a 3,200-foot tunnel in the Contra Costa hills just east of Oakland; and a Key System ferry trip across San Francisco Bay (or, starting in January 1939, direct rail service from Oakland to San Francisco on the bottom deck of the newly built Bay Bridge).

The northern half of the railway line started with the incorporation of the Northern Electric Railway in 1905. The Northern Electric was reorganized as the Sacramento Northern Railroad in 1918. The Sacramento Northern Railroad merged with the San Francisco–Sacramento Railway in 1928 and was thereafter known as the Sacramento Northern Railway. This railway line had a single Placer County station in the town of Riego, in the extreme southwest corner of the county. Many people who are very knowledgeable about the Sacramento Northern Railway are not aware of the fact that Riego was in Placer County and that the system had a Placer County connection. Even many people who live in Placer County and Sutter County do not know about Riego or think that Riego is located in Sutter County. The second image appearing in this chapter is of a small portion of a map of Placer County showing Riego's location and how the Sacramento Northern Railway's tracks passed right through the small community.

Though small and isolated in the southwest corner of Placer County, the town's location on the Sacramento Northern Railway encouraged plans for the development of Riego due to the available transportation and shipping options that the railway provided. One such development plan was a proposal by a Sacramento automobile company in 1911 to build a large automobile factory on a tract of land at Riego. However, the Sacramento automobile company never followed through on its plans.

As with many of the stops along the system, Riego was a flag stop, which means a person had to notify the system that a passenger car needed to stop to pick up or drop off passengers. The stops out in the sparsely populated areas along the railway system's route had small buildings designed only to provide shelter from the elements. There was no need to have a ticket agent at these stops, as a passenger would purchase a ticket from a conductor aboard the railway cars. Buying a ticket from the onboard conductor was the same method people used to ride the cars within the cities, where the railway system had tracks laid in the streets.

The entire Sacramento Northern Railway system is shown on this map. The only Placer County stop on this system is at Riego, which can be seen about five stops north of Sacramento. (Western Railroad Museum Archives.)

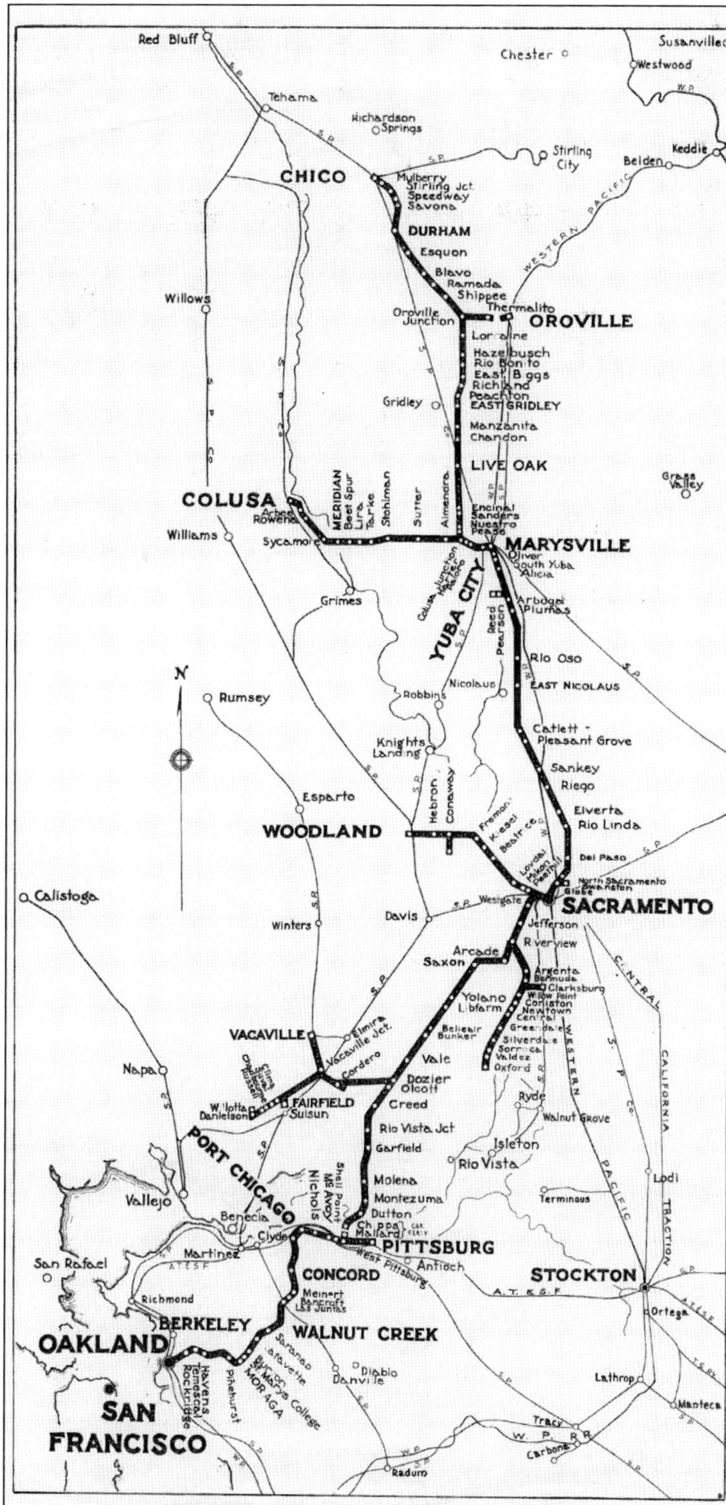

SACRAMENTO NORTHERN RAILWAY

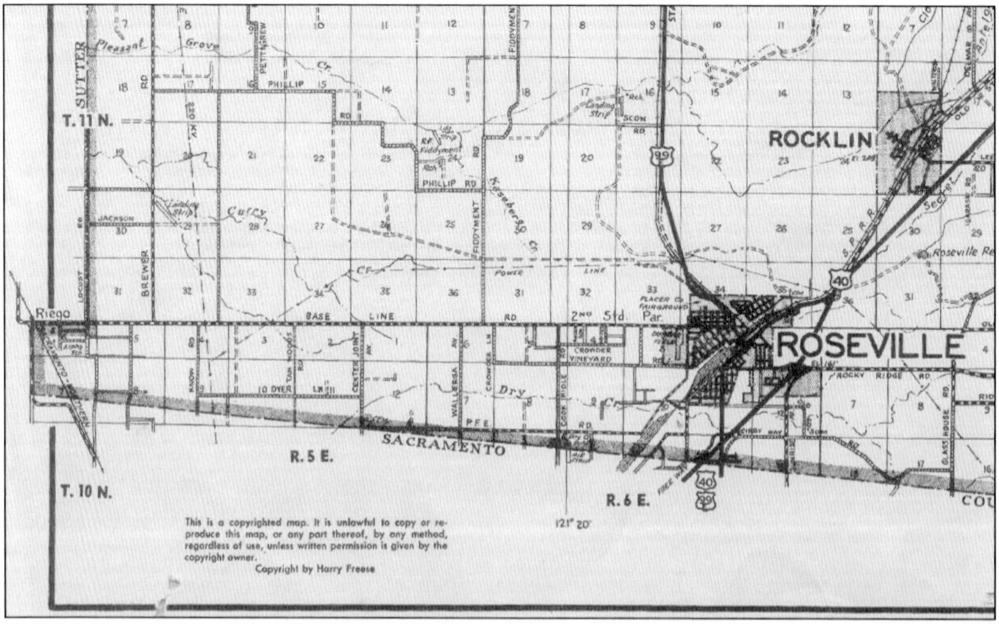

This map shows why the Sacramento Northern Railway is included in this book of railroads in Placer County. The map indicates that the Sacramento Northern Railway line crossed into Placer County at the small community of Riego, shown at the extreme left edge. Placer County has an odd bump of land sticking out in its most extreme southwest corner. Riego was the only stop in Placer County for the Sacramento Northern. (PSRHS.)

The northern half of the 180 miles of the Sacramento Northern Railway got its start in 1905 as the Northern Electric. This photograph shows a bridge being built across the American River in Sacramento County to allow Northern Electric trains to cross from Sacramento to reach the towns of Riego, Marysville, Yuba City, and ultimately Chico. (AJS.)

The authors were unable to locate a photograph of the building at Riego used by passengers waiting for a Sacramento Northern electric car, but images for nearby stops are shown on this page. The image above shows the stop at Del Paso just across the American River from Sacramento. The image below shows the stop at Elverta, which was the stop just south of Riego. The buildings at most of the Sacramento Northern stops were small, as they were meant only to provide waiting passengers shelter from the weather. People purchased tickets from the conductor onboard. (Both, Western Railroad Museum Archives.)

The Sacramento Northern was an electric-powered railway system, thus each car could travel independently or be hooked together with other cars to form a train. This image shows three cars together on the northern half of the route. A passenger waiting at Riego might have boarded this train. (Western Railroad Museum Archives.)

An individual car is crossing the bridge over the Yuba River near Marysville. The car seen in this image and the ones in the previous image have their overhead power poles and pantograph folded down across the top of the car, as the system used a third rail to provide power on most of the northern half of the system. (Western Railroad Museum Archives.)

The Sacramento Northern's steeple cab locomotive No. 654 has its pantograph extended up to the overhead power lines. These types of locomotives were used to pull freight trains, as the boxcars and flatcars making up those freight trains were not individually powered, unlike the dedicated passenger cars built for the Sacramento Northern Railway. (AJS.)

In 1937, Sacramento Northern car No. 1004 had a run-in with a truck loaded with rice harvested from the farms that were abundant in the flatlands surrounding Riego and other stops heading north. (AJS.)

FESTIVITIES LAST SATURDAY.

Railroad Company's Barbecue Attracts Many Strangers—Exercises at the Opera House.

Last Saturday the much advertised barbecue, given by the Auburn Electric Railroad Company, came off. It was given to celebrate the completion of the laying of the road-bed from the depot to the postoffice. Many people from the surrounding country and nearby towns were present to partake of the "great feast." Until 12 o'clock people asked each other and wondered where the barbecue would take place and at what time. Nobody seemed to know. But round the vacant lot adjoining Breslin's shop was a small crowd watching Cook Brown roasting the meat. Whither they all went. The meat was cut into small strips and placed on the rails over the hot coals. About 2 o'clock the feast was ready, and many partook thereof. After the barbecue exercises were held on the plaza, where the golden spike was driven. Four little girls, beautifully attired, each with a little silver hammer, with alternate strokes drove the golden spike into the wood. The little misses were Irene Bisbee, Cora Connors, Frances Snowden and Agnes Walsh. After the spike was driven A. K. Robinson delivered a short address. His remarks were good and were appreciated by his listeners.

In the evening exercises were held at the Opera House. Addresses were made by R. F. Burns, W. B. Lardner and L. L. Chamberlain, and a piece was recited by Mrs. Guy Walsh. H. H. Richmond presided. The prettiest feature of the whole day's exercises was the minuet, danced by four pairs of Auburn's best dancers. The ladies looked very beautiful and the gentlemen appeared well.

After the minuet a dance was held in Kenison's hall, in which over a hundred couples participated. There was a very large number of visitors in town, although it might have been a little premature to celebrate. However, the president of the railroad seems quite well satisfied with the day.

A newspaper article from a 1901 issue of the *Placer Herald* shows that electric-powered railroads were all the rage across the country around the turn of the century. Many cities came to operate their own independent electric railway systems. A rather obscure piece of Placer County railroad history is the fact that the city of Auburn (the seat of Placer County) nearly had an electric-powered railroad running right through the center of town from the railroad depot past the Placer County Courthouse to the post office. Auburn's electric-powered railroad company was incorporated in December 1900. The company laid wooden ties and steel rails down the center of the main street in Auburn. By August 1901, the company stated that it intended to extend the line out to nearby Bowman. A "golden spike" ceremony was held on Saturday, October 5, 1901, in Central Square, as reported in the *Placer Herald* article shown at left. However, before the Auburn Electric Railroad Company could purchase rolling stock to make the railroad operational, it went bankrupt in January 1902, only months after the "golden spike" ceremony. By February 1902, the steel rails were sold and removed, though the wooden ties were left in place and covered with a thin layer of dirt. For 10 years, people complained of the bone-jarring ride that the wooden ties inflicted on travelers. Finally, in August 1912, the *Placer Herald* reported that the city planned a street improvement project to remove the wooden ties and grade the road to smooth it out. (AJS.)

Five

Mountain Quarries Railroad

A large-scale limestone mining operation by the Mountain Quarries Company was started on the El Dorado County side of the Middle Fork of the American River in 1909. The operation eventually included three separate mining pits, tunnels, a crushing plant for the limestone, and a seven-mile-long standard-gauge rail line with locomotives and gondola cars to haul the limestone. Though only seven miles long, the railroad crossed the American River over an impressive concrete bridge into Placer County and also traversed 17 wooden trestles. Palmer, McBride, and Quail was the contractor for building the roadbed. On March 23, 1912, the railroad was officially opened for business. Shortly after that, the Pacific Portland Cement Company bought out the Mountain Quarries Company and assumed control of the limestone mining operation and of the railroad. The large-scale mining of limestone at the Mountain Quarries site ended in 1941, and the steel rails used by the railroad operations were torn up the following year as scrap metal for the World War II war effort. Profitable mining of limestone is still carried out at the upper section of the deposit, and the limestone is now hauled out by trucks.

After leaving the loading site at Mountain Quarries, the limestone-laden railcars were moved to the concrete bridge. From there, only three to four cars at a time could be pulled up the steep grade, over the trestles, and through a switchback, to the top of the canyon on the Placer County side of the American River. There, the cars loaded with limestone were readied to be transferred to the Southern Pacific Railroad mainline at SP's Flint Station. Flint Station was located on the outskirts of Auburn on Gold Street, just above the Placer High School campus. In 1938, the State Relief Agency and the Works Progress Administration established Camp Flint. On December 9, 1941 (only two days after the Japanese bombing of Pearl Harbor), the Army moved troops into the Camp Flint facility. In 1945, the camp was used as a prisoner-of-war camp, with the POWs assigned to help at the nearby DeWitt Army Hospital.

John Leonard was the architect who designed the Mountain Quarries Bridge. The bridge was started in 1910, when a construction crew of over 800 men was hired to begin work on what would be at the time the longest reinforced concrete railroad bridge in the world. The work crew was divided into two groups, with 200 men working from one side, while 600 worked from the other. A large concrete manufacturing facility was built on the banks of the American River right at the bridge construction site. In approximately two years, the bridge and the rest of the railroad were completed. When automobile traffic became more prevalent, this railroad was one of the few that actually had to yield to automobile traffic, instead of the other way around. The railroad crossed Highway 49 upstream from the Mountain Quarries Bridge on the El Dorado County side of the canyon.

Because the Mountain Quarries Bridge was constructed solely for the purpose of allowing the trains to cross the American River, no guardrails or handrails were built. After the railroad shut down, people walking and riding horseback across the bridge came to call it No Hands Bridge. The bridge survived the war's scrap metal drives because it was made out of concrete. Mountain Quarries Bridge is famous today as the means for horses and riders to cross the river during the annual Tevis Cup ride as well as the Western States Endurance Run, which uses the same 100-mile-long trail, but that race is run by humans.

The limestone at the Mountain Quarries site was of a very high grade in a ledge whose direction generally ran north-south. The limestone was hauled out of the mine in six-ton cars from the bottom up to a crusher. After this initial crushing, the limestone was passed through huge screens into bins. From those bins, the limestone was drawn through another crusher. The results of that second crush were sent on conveyor belts to storage bunkers. The crushed limestone was then ready to be loaded into gondola cars for transportation to Flint Station at Auburn and then ultimately to the kilns at the Pacific Portland Cement Company's operation at Cement, California. Cement was a company town near Fairfield in Solano County. There is no town anymore; the site can be reached using Cement Hill Road. The site was in the hills on the northwest boundary of present-day Travis Air Force Base. The area has now been turned into a housing development. The mines and processing plant at Cement opened in 1900, were enlarged in 1903, and were enlarged again in 1905. An entirely new plant was built and began operations in 1907. The limestone was running out at the Cement site, and thus the new limestone being shipped in from the Mountain Quarries site was welcome.

Before large-scale limestone mining was implemented at the Mountain Quarries site, the area was known for a large cave containing ice-age fossils. An Auburn dentist, photographer, and amateur paleontologist, Dr. John C. Hawver made the cave famous in the early 20th century when he reported finding fossils inside. Fossils from the Hawver Cave, including skulls and bones of the saber-tooth cat, ground sloth, mammoth, and bison, are on display at the Sierra College Natural History Museum in Rocklin, California.

The *Placer Herald* of Saturday, July 1, 1911, includes this article on the progress being made on construction work for the Mountain Quarries Railroad and mining operations at the quarry site. The article mentions that 14 trestles are being built. The actual number of trestles was 17 by the time construction work was finished. (AJS.)

Mountain Quarries Railroad

Work on the Mountain Quarries railroad is going on with a rush. 600 men are working on the Placer and 200 on the El Dorado side of the American river and a large force at the quarry. The latter is running a tunnel, getting out limestone and preparing sites for the mill and other buildings.

The railroad will cross the Georgetown wagon road just above the wire bridge and thence cross the river about 600 feet below that bridge on a three-span re-enforced concrete bridge 170 feet long. It will continue down the river to the Nierhoff ranch south of Auburn, where it will turn and be extended up the Rich Flat Gulch to the Flat which will be used as a yard.

The ravines will be crossed on fourteen trestles, the longest of which will be the one crossing the ravine leading from the Auburn depot. This trestle will be 70 feet high and 700 feet long.

The work of running cuts and filling swales is progressing rapidly and the road will be completed within a year. Its length will be seven miles. Ex-Sheriff W. A. Conroy is field man and is kept busy overseeing the many construction gangs.

Dr. John C. Hawver took this photograph of the limestone quarry in 1907. At that time, all that could be seen was this outcropping and some small-scale mining done to obtain limestone. This was the site of the Hawver Cave and soon to be the site of large-scale mining by the Mountain Quarries Company. (AJS.)

A decade after Dr. Hawver's photograph was taken, the Mountain Quarries mining operation was in full swing, as evidenced by the huge, gaping wound in the side of the hill along the Middle Fork of the American River. The crushing mill and the loading conveyer belts at the terminus of the Mountain Quarries Railroad are seen at bottom center of this image. (AJS.)

The Mountain Quarry is just on the other side of hill where the two roads curve around to the right. The roadbed at bottom left is for the Mountain Quarries Railroad, while the roadbed at right is the wagon road into the mining site. Placer County is across the river, while the quarry was located in El Dorado County. (AJS.)

Scaffolding used to build the Mountain Quarries Bridge across the American River is in place for pouring the concrete. On November 4, 1911, one of the arches collapsed with 20 workers on it. Three men were killed and five more injured seriously. The remaining men suffered only minor injuries. (AJS.)

The 600-foot-long bridge was completed by March 1912, but in this image, some scaffolding can still be seen at the tops of two arches. At the same time this railroad bridge was being built at the bottom of the American River canyon for the Mountain Quarries Railroad, Southern Pacific was building a steel railroad bridge across the Auburn Ravine just outside Auburn in support of that railroad's double-tracking effort (see page 46). (AJS.)

Wooden ties and steel rails have been laid across the bridge. The old suspension bridge can be seen upstream in the distance. That bridge was on the Georgetown Road, as it was known in those days. That road became Highway 49, and the suspension bridge was replaced with a modern bridge. The modern Highway 49 bridge was completely destroyed during a flood in December 1964. (AJS.)

A horse-drawn wagon is parked on the suspension bridge. The Mountain Quarries Bridge can be seen downstream. One of the many trestles built for the Mountain Quarries Railroad can be seen in the upper left corner of the photograph. (AJS.)

Nine fully loaded gondola cars are shown on the Mountain Quarries Bridge. The railroad grade allowed the locomotive to pull that many cars to the bridge, but the grade was too steep to go much farther, so some of the loaded cars were separated from the train. The locomotive would haul some to Flint and return to get the rest. (AJS.)

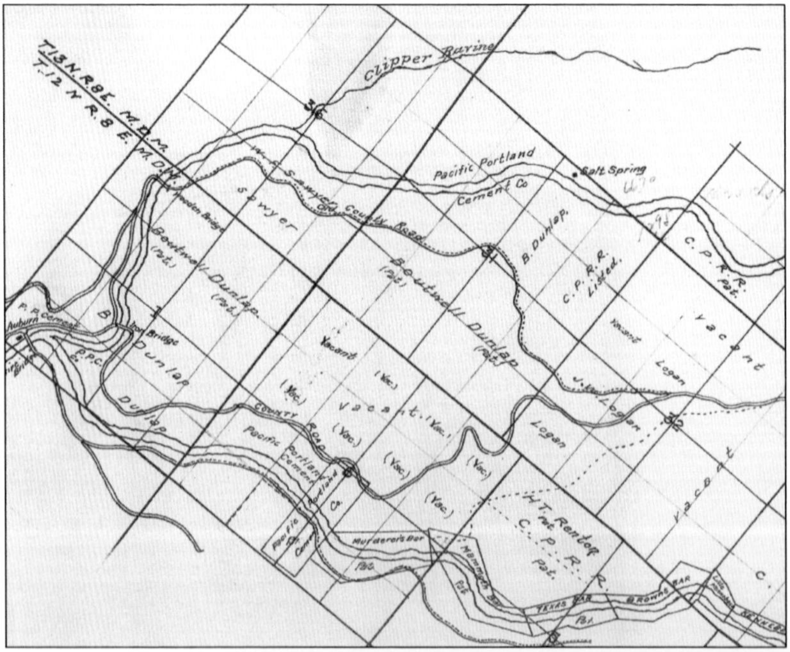

This survey map from 1912 shows the area where the North Fork and Middle Fork of the American River merge at the left margin. The map also shows the Pacific Portland Cement (PPC) Company owning many plots of land. PPC's Mountain Quarries site is at bottom center, adjacent to the Murderer's Bar gold-mining claim. (AJS.)

This modern aerial photograph shows the same area as the survey map at the top of this page. Bridge 1 is the modern bridge to Foresthill, built when there were plans to build the Auburn Dam, which would have flooded the area, forming a new lake. Bridge 2 is the old bridge to Foresthill. Bridge 3 is the Highway 49 bridge linking Placer County with El Dorado County. Bridge 4 is the Mountain Quarries Railroad bridge. (Mike Lynch.)

The Mountain Quarries Railroad climbed the canyon wall of the American River. Trains had to maneuver this switchback to reach the top of the canyon and transfer the loaded gondola cars to the Southern Pacific Railroad mainline at Flint Station. (AJS.)

A locomotive is pushing the loaded gondola cars up the final grade. At the switchback between these two trestles, the locomotive pulled the cars onto a spur then backed up the track to Flint, pushing the cars to the top of the grade. (Ken Yeo.)

Derailments were the bane of railroads around the world. In this photograph, a crane is attempting to lift the derailed boxcar back up onto the tracks at the Mountain Quarries Railroad switchback near the top of the American River canyon. (AJS.)

The locomotive has delivered its loaded cars to the transfer station at Flint and is now backing down to the bridge to pick up more cars filled with limestone. This photograph was taken in 1940. (Ken Yeo.)

Pacific Portland Cement Company Consolidated locomotive No. 102 is parked at Flint Station. This photograph was taken on July 19, 1937. This 2-8-2-configuration locomotive was built by the Baldwin Locomotive Works, which manufactured over 70,000 locomotives from the 1830s to the 1950s. (AJS.)

During World War II, the US Army occupied the camp at Flint Station. It was known as Camp Flint. The soldiers stationed at Camp Flint were to guard the rail lines, which were vital for the transportation of war materials. Later in the war, the camp was also used to house German and Italian POWs. (Placer County Museum.)

This view looks across the top of the old suspension bridge and downstream to the Mountain Quarries Bridge. The water level in the river here is at the normal height. The mountain rivers in Northern California flooded most winters. (AJS.)

The American River is at flood stage due to runoff from rains and snowmelt. The water can be seen passing under the Mountain Quarries Bridge with a lot of clearance. (AJS.)

In December 1964, the Hell Hole Dam on the Middle Fork of the American River failed and the waters behind the dam came rushing down the riverbed. In this photograph, the floodwaters are pushing against the modern steel bridge built for the Highway 49 crossing. Downstream, there is still some clearance between the river waters and the arches of the Mountain Quarries Bridge. (AJS.)

The continued force of the raging floodwaters was too much for the Highway 49 bridge. This photograph was taken just as it collapsed from the tremendous pressure of the water. The much older Mountain Quarries concrete bridge survived the 1964 flood and was pressed into service as an automobile bridge until the collapsed Highway 49 bridge could be replaced. (AJS.)

Another photograph shows a locomotive pulling a train of four loaded cars up to the top of the American River canyon to drop them off at the Flint transfer station. The loaded cars would be transferred to the Southern Pacific mainline for delivery to Cement, California, in Solano County. (Ken Yeo.)

The ultimate destination for the cars loaded with Mountain Quarries limestone was the kilns at Cement. The Pacific Portland Cement Company's mills and kilns were originally used to process the limestone mined on-site at Cement, but as the limestone began to peter out there, high-quality limestone was brought in from the company's Mountain Quarries site. (AJS.)

Six

Nevada County Narrow Gauge Railroad

The primary objective in building the transcontinental railroad was to connect California with the rest of the country. But as the new railroad pushed into Placer County, it provided improved service to nearby mining areas in the Sierra foothills. After tracks reached Colfax, passengers and supplies heading for the mining communities of Grass Valley and Nevada City in Nevada County were off-loaded in Colfax then completed their journey by wagon or coach. One early newspaper account of an 1873 journey noted that the 54-mile train trip from Sacramento to Colfax went very smoothly. However, the 20-mile coach ride on the dirt road to Grass Valley was tedious. The relatively short distance from Colfax to Grass Valley took three and a half hours on the winding, zigzag route. Delivery of heavy equipment for the mines was often hampered by mud or snow on the poor roads.

A group of Nevada County businessmen noted the problem and decided to build a narrow-gauge railroad from the Central Pacific tracks at Colfax to Grass Valley and Nevada City. In May 1876, the Nevada County Narrow Gauge Railroad (NCNG) began providing scheduled passenger and freight service on the 20-mile run. The new railroad left Colfax on tracks that paralleled the Central Pacific tracks to Long Ravine. There, the NCNG went under the Central Pacific's Long Ravine Bridge, crossed Long Ravine and the Bear River at today's Rollins Lake, then paralleled today's Highway 174 and Brunswick and Bennett Roads to Grass Valley before continuing to Nevada City. At Colfax, NCNG passengers boarded on the opposite side of the depot from where Central Pacific and later Southern Pacific passengers boarded. In 1881, a 270-foot-long transfer shed was built at one end of the Colfax Freight Depot for transferring freight from narrow-gauge to standard-gauge railcars.

NCNG tracks originally crossed the Bear River from Placer County to Nevada County on a wooden bridge and trestle. The bridge and part of the trestle were destroyed by fire in 1896, and the bridge was rebuilt with a wooden structure that could withstand heavier loads. John Kidder served as superintendent of the NCNG from its initial construction, and he became president of the line in 1884. When he died in 1901, his wife, Sara Kidder, became president of the NCNG, a role she held for 12 years that are referred to as the golden years.

During Sara Kidder's reign, a cutoff was built in 1908 that relocated the line between Long Ravine and Chicago Park. This realignment had been envisioned and surveyed by John Kidder and George Fletcher in the 1890s, before Kidder's death. The main feature of this change was a 173-foot-high steel bridge that crossed the Bear River from Placer County to Nevada County, along with a new steel viaduct over Long Ravine in Placer County. This new cutoff eliminated wooden trestles at Bear River, Greenhorn Creek, and Shebley's.

The NCNG operated up to three scheduled trains daily, though its frequent schedule delays earned it the nickname "Never Come Never Go." It also provided excursion trains and moonlight runs to a picnic area and dance pavilion near Chicago Park. As years went by, passenger ridership dropped on the line, and the NCNG began replacing passenger trains between Colfax and Grass Valley and Nevada City with rail motor car and bus service. During World War II, the local mines were deemed nonessential to the war effort, and the Grass Valley and Nevada City mines were unable to get the supplies they needed for their operations. These restrictions greatly reduced the freight business for the railroad, with the result that the NCNG railroad ceased operations in 1942. Some of its equipment was sold, while its tracks were torn up and sold for scrap value.

Remnants of the right-of-way are still visible at several locations along Highway 174. The high bridge over the Bear River remained visible from Highway 174 until 1963, when it was torn down to make way for construction of Rollins Dam. In a testament to the bridge's construction, dynamite failed to bring it down. It took cutting torches and tractors with cables to finally remove this highly visible remnant of the once-proud Nevada County Narrow Gauge Railroad.

This map shows the route of the NCNG over its 20-mile trek, starting in Colfax in Placer County, crossing the Bear River on a wooden trestle and bridge into Nevada County, and continuing to Grass Valley and Nevada City. In 1908, the railroad line was rerouted to bypass some troublesome grades. The old Bear River crossing was replaced by a high steel bridge that crossed the Bear River farther downstream, then met the original line near Chicago Park. (PSRHS.)

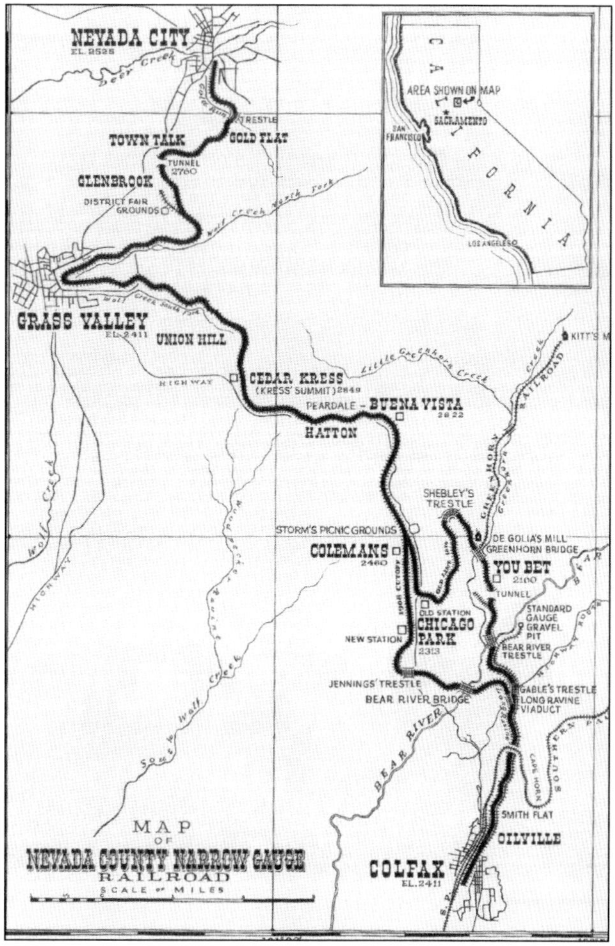

In Colfax, the NCNG tracks and Central Pacific tracks (Southern Pacific after about 1901) were on opposite sides of the passenger depot. This early view looks across the depot platform from the Central Pacific tracks at a NCNG train with its passenger cars. The depot building is at the far left, and at right is the Wells Fargo building. Beyond the train is the Central Hotel, which served rail passengers until it was destroyed by fire in 1901. (AJS.)

In 1905 a new SP passenger depot was built in Colfax at its present-day location. Passengers dressed in their traveling finery are waiting next to the depot to board the NCNG train on tracks that ran behind the depot on what is now Railroad Avenue. The open-air car was used for excursions. (PSRHS.)

An NCNG train that includes a combination baggage/passenger car and a passenger coach waits on the tracks near the Colfax Depot. NCNG trains often included freight cars and transported both passengers and freight to and from Grass Valley and Nevada City. (AJS.)

This is a closer view of the NCNG combination baggage/passenger car near the Colfax Depot. The Colfax Hotel can be seen in the background. This car was delivered to the NCNG in May 1876 and rebuilt in 1890. The NCNG had three of these combination cars. (AJS.)

The image at right shows the simple but comfortable-looking interior of a passenger coach. The cushions on the center floor indicate that the coach may be undergoing cleaning or modifications. (Ken Yeo.)

In 1907, Nevada County officials erected a quartz monument in Colfax between the SP and NCNG tracks near the depot. The purpose was to inform visitors of gold-mining activity in Nevada County, accessible on NCNG trains. Above, the monument is under construction with a NCNG train at right, SP tracks at lower right, and the Gillen (later Colfax) Hotel at left. Below, a plaque visible on the completed Nevada County Exhibit provides information on Nevada County gold mining. The building at left behind the monument is the Marvin Hotel, which burned in 1939. In 1914, the monument was moved to a spot in front of the Marvin Hotel due to SP track realignment. The monument survived until the mid-1920s. (Both, AJS.)

Colfax was a very active railroad town when the NCNG was still in business. At lower right in this 1912 image, an NCNG train is waiting to depart the Colfax Depot, which is just out of view at left. In the center is a Southern Pacific passenger train stopped next to the Wells Fargo/Railway Express building. The freight depot is the building at the extreme right, past the quartz monument. Beyond the freight depot was a transfer shed for moving freight between SP and NCNG freight cars. (AJS.)

This view shows NCNG motor car No. 1 in the Colfax yard. The railroad line experimented with several gas-fueled motor cars starting around 1907. They were built or modified in the Grass Valley shops and were used for excursions and to meet special trains in Colfax. The motor cars often were on call, essentially operating as rail taxis. In the 1930s, the NCNG began to use buses for some of the passenger traffic from Colfax, and in 1938, it ceased offering rail passenger service but continued rail freight service and passenger buses. (Ken Yeo.)

NCNG No. 5 is shown performing switching duties at Colfax. This locomotive has the distinction of being perhaps the NCNG's most famous. When the NCNG began selling off its assets, No. 5 was sold to what became Universal Studios in Los Angeles, where it appeared in numerous movies and television shows. In 1985, it was brought back to Nevada County, and it now resides at the Nevada County Narrow Gauge Railroad Museum in Nevada City. (Andrew Brandon.)

NCNG No. 8 is being rotated on the Colfax turntable for the return trip to Grass Valley. The turntable was next to the narrow-gauge tracks just past the highway bridge and Oilville, at the north edge of town. It served the NCNG from 1915 to 1942. The turntable pit remained until it was removed for construction of Interstate 80. (Ken Yeo.)

After leaving Colfax, the NCNG tracks seen at far right began to slowly diverge away from the main line tracks and started a gradual descent that took NCNG trains under the main line's Long Ravine Bridge. At lower right is Oilville, where fuel oil was transferred to NCNG trains. The turntable is barely visible at upper right. This view is from the highway bridge. The following image shows this same location but in a view from track level looking back towards Colfax. (AJS.)

In this Al Phelps photograph, NCNG No. 9 pulls its train out of Colfax toward Grass Valley, passing under the Highway 40 (now Highway 174) bridge. To the left of the tracks are the pipes at Oilville used to transfer fuel oil to NCNG trains. To take on fuel, the locomotive backed down the grade in the foreground below the pipes. (Ken Yeo.)

When the Central Pacific was first built, Long Ravine was crossed by a wooden trestle and bridge. This c. 1886 view, taken by William Perkins, shows a Central Pacific train on the wooden bridge at Long Ravine, with an early NCNG train and its crew posed on the narrow-gauge tracks below the bridge. (Andrew Brandon.)

The Central Pacific knew its wooden Long Ravine Bridge would need to be replaced in the 1880s. Railroad officials seriously considered filling in the ravine, which would have required the NCNG to build a tunnel through the fill. But instead of fill, the wooden bridge was replaced with an iron bridge. Central Pacific's new Long Ravine Bridge, or Viaduct, was completed in 1890. The water tank was known as the Smith Flat tank. (AJS.)

NCNG tracks originally crossed the Bear River into Nevada County on a wooden bridge and curved wooden trestle, shown in these two images. A similar wooden bridge and trestle crossed Greenhorn Creek. The Bear River bridge and a portion of the trestle shown below were destroyed by fire in 1896 but were rebuilt. (Both, Ken Yeo.)

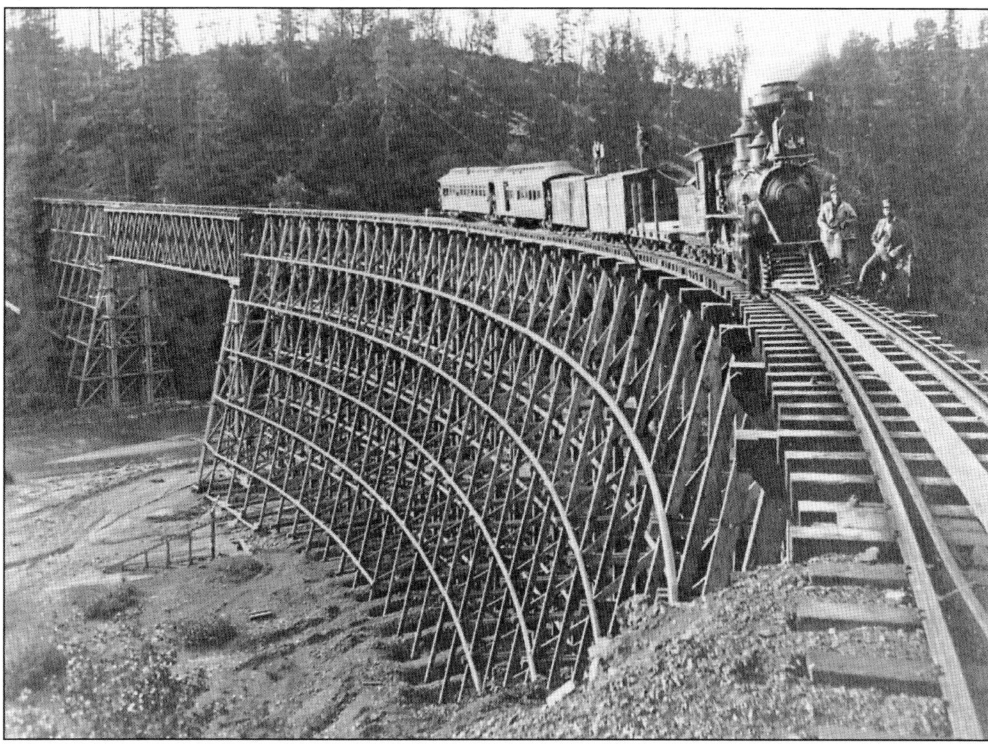

In 1907, NCNG officials began building a cutoff that had been surveyed during John Kidder's reign. A new and higher crossing of the Bear River was established further downstream that reduced the railroad grades and eliminated three wooden bridges and a tunnel. A new steel bridge was built just below the location of present-day Rollins Lake Dam. A viaduct was also built to cross Long Ravine at a higher elevation. In the photograph above, an NCNG train is seen crossing the new 173-foot-high Bear River Bridge. Below, the Long Ravine Viaduct crossed the ravine and later Highway 40 roughly where Rollins Lake Road now meets the lake. The highway grade in this photograph is now beneath the waters of Rollins Lake. Old concrete piers for the viaduct and a highway culvert are visible when the lake level is low. (Both, Ken Yeo.)

A long mixed freight and passenger train is heading toward Colfax on Jennings Trestle. This trestle crossed the open meadow area between Chicago Park and the Bear River on the 1908 cutoff. The trestle was named for the landowner who gave permission to build it on his property. Both scenes on this page are located in Nevada County. (Ken Yeo.)

The NCNG paralleled what is now Highway 174 from Chicago Park to the Cedar Ridge Wye, then called Cedar Kress. This photograph has a view looking towards Colfax at Cedar Kress. Today, a market, restaurant, and other businesses are located in the area to the right of the road. (Ken Yeo.)

Back in Colfax, NCNG No. 9 and its freight cars are moving along Railroad Avenue next to the Pacific Fruit Exchange sheds. After the Southern Pacific tracks were realigned in Colfax in 1915, the shed for transferring cargo between SP and NCNG cars was moved to the Colfax yard in the distance, beyond the fruit sheds. (PSRHS.)

The NCNG found its revenue dropping off in the early days of World War II, due in part to wartime restrictions on mining activities and other businesses. Railroad officials soon found that the railroad was worth more as scrap metal than as an operating railroad and decided to cease operations. In 1943, a scrap train and crew started in Nevada City on its way to Colfax, pulling up rail and collecting other metal as it went. In this Al Phelps photograph, dated April 24, 1943, the scrap train and crew are removing the metal rails at the outskirts of Colfax in the shadow of the Highway 40 (now 174) bridge. (Ken Yeo.)

Seven

Towle Brothers Narrow Gauge Railroad

This chapter covers two once-thriving narrow-gauge logging railroads owned by Towle Brothers Company and later Read Lumber Company.

In the mid-19th century, the Towle Brothers Company was building a logging and lumber business in Placer County. In the 1870s, the company leased property from the Central Pacific Railroad on either side of the CPRR's main line tracks just east of Alta in Placer County. The Towle Brothers Company built a company town on that leased property. In addition, it bought property outright in support of the community. The community of Towle became a site for processing logs and rough-cut lumber brought in from the outlying property northeast of Towle. Towle Brothers built its own narrow-gauge railroad extending from Towle out into the countryside, eventually crossing the Bear River into Nevada County. The narrow-gauge line followed a very convoluted route for 30 miles throughout the area's hills and valleys, crossing many creeks and streams. Those crossings required numerous wooden trestles to be built in support of the railroad. Because the Towle Brothers Company was mainly a lumber company, obtaining sufficient timbers to build the trestles was not an obstacle. By the summer of 1885, the rolling stock of the railroad consisted of 60 flatcars and four narrow-gauge locomotives. It later acquired a fifth narrow-gauge locomotive.

In the 1880s, the Towle Brothers Lumber Company established a sawmill on heavily forested land farther east of Towle and about four miles due south of Emigrant Gap, in an area of rural Placer County known as Texas Hill. Cut lumber was transported from the company's Texas Hill sawmill to the Central Pacific tracks near Emigrant Gap using oxen-drawn wagons and later steam tractors. Into the 1890s, Towle Brothers continued to log parts of Nevada County at the far reaches of its narrow-gauge railroad and transported the lumber products back to Towle. Meanwhile, it was expanding its operations at Texas Hill. In 1899, the company made the decision to shut down the Nevada County operations. It dismantled its 30-mile, narrow-gauge railroad that ran from Towle and shifted all the logging and lumber operations to the area near Texas Hill. Towle Brothers built a larger sawmill at the top of Texas Hill and moved its remaining lumber businesses from Towle to Fulda Flat, a few miles west of Emigrant Gap on the CPRR. By early 1902, Towle Brothers had rebuilt its narrow-gauge railroad to move lumber from their mills at Texas Hill to the yard at Fulda Flat.

In August 1902, the Read Lumber Company of Canada bought Towle Brothers' Texas Hill logging operations, including the narrow-gauge railroad and all the lumber businesses at Fulda Flat. Over the next two decades, the Read Company expanded the Texas Hill logging and lumber operations. It built two incline tracks at Texas Hill—one to hoist carloads of logs to the mill at the top of the hill and another to lower carloads of cut lumber to the base of the hill for transport on its narrow-gauge railroad to Fulda Flat. In 1920, Read Lumber sold its Texas Hill and Fulda Flat operations and equipment, including the narrow-gauge railroad, when the marketable timber in the area became depleted.

Towle Brothers Company retained ownership of land and buildings at the town of Towle, but with the lumber business at Towle no longer operating, the town began a steady decline. Today, other than nearby Towle Road, there is nothing left at the old townsite as a reminder of the bustling lumber town that once stood there.

The two images on this page show the use of oxen to pull the cut trees out of the forest back to a mill for processing. Though relatively effective, the use of oxen was just not sufficient for a large-scale logging business. The Towle Brothers Company was one of the largest lumber businesses in Northern California during the last half of the 19th century. (AJS.)

Towle Brothers' solution to increasing the efficiency of its logging business was to build a narrow-gauge railroad to supplement and eventually replace the use of oxen for moving cut trees and processed lumber around its property, which consisted of over 19,000 acres in 1885. (AJS.)

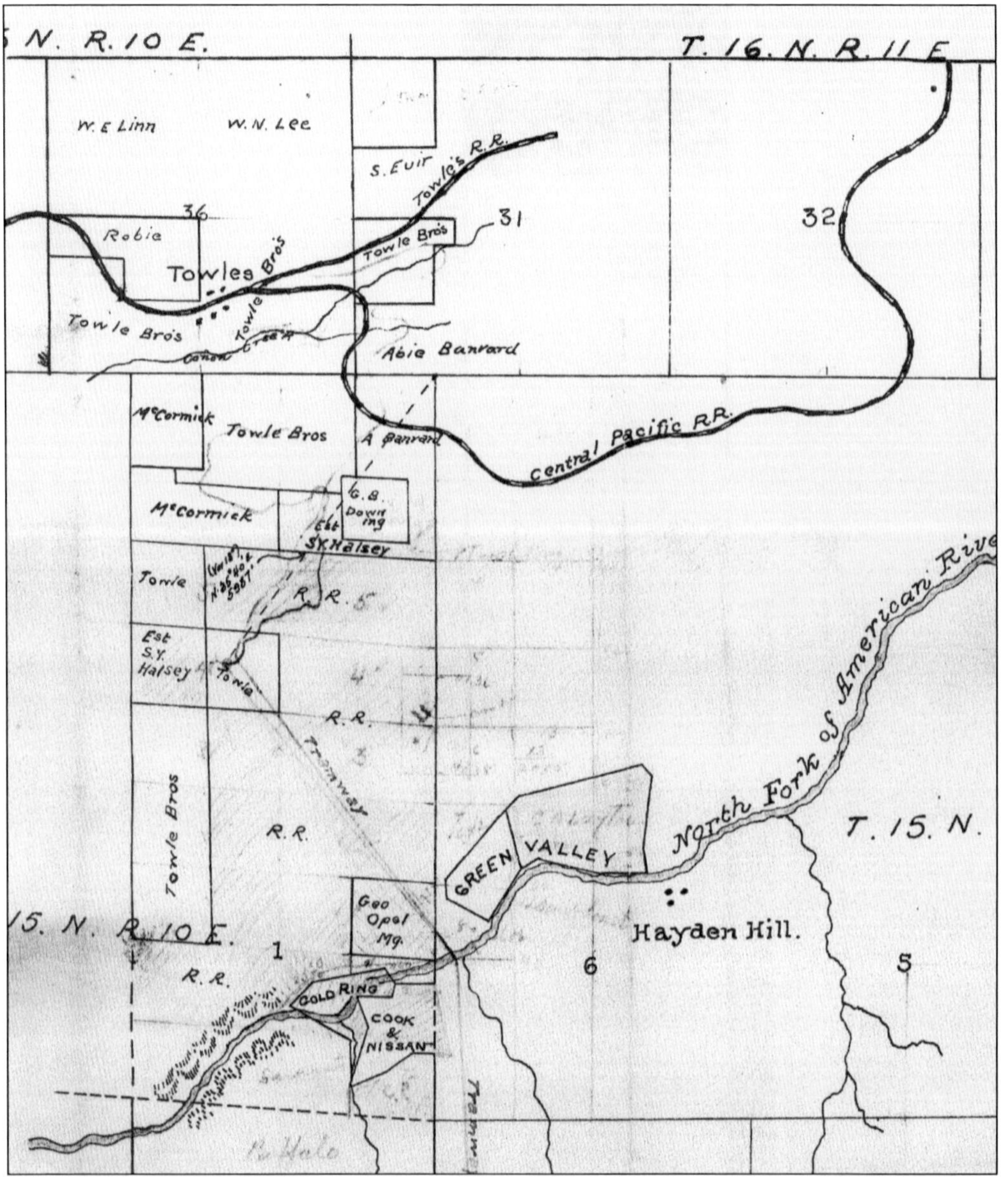

A property ownership survey map shows the community of Towle in the upper left corner. The Central Pacific Railroad leaves Towle and makes a big curve to the southeast, while the Towle Brothers Narrow Gauge tracks leave Towle heading to the northeast. The Towle Brothers Company had retail lumber dealerships in many towns in Placer County, including Auburn, Lincoln, Newcastle, Rocklin, and Roseville, as well as Wheatland in Yuba County and Grass Valley and Nevada City in Nevada County. All those dealerships had retail locations adjacent to railroad tracks to facilitate the shipment of lumber from Towle to the retail dealers. (AJS.)

A bird's-eye view of the Towle area shows the Central Pacific Railroad main line leaving Towle and curving off to the left at the bottom of the image. The Towle Brothers Narrow Gauge line ran right through the middle of the stacks of drying lumber, seen at the right side of the image. (AJS.)

This image shows the Towle station building on the left with the "Towle" sign sticking up from the roofline. A cab-forward locomotive is belching smoke. The roof of the two-story Towle store is seen right over the top of the locomotive. It was this thick smoke being trapped inside 30 miles of snowsheds over Donner Summit that led to the cab-forward design, putting the engineers' cab in front of the locomotive's smoky exhaust. (AJS.)

Two young girls are playing at Towle. The main line railroad tracks run right behind them and in front of the Towle store. The tall pole at the corner of the store was used to signal the trains. The Towle Brothers Narrow Gauge Railroad tracks run behind the store. (AJS.)

Some of the Towle Brothers Railroad flatcars are loaded up with company workers in preparation for a trip out into the countryside for a Fourth of July picnic in 1882. The flatcars are on the narrow-gauge tracks running behind the Towle store. The Central Pacific Railroad main line tracks are on the far side of the store building. Two boxcars can be seen on the CPRR tracks just over the heads of the waiting picnic participants. (AJS.)

Numerous narrow-gauge tracks lead right into lumber processing sheds at Towle. A locomotive can be seen in the opening of the shed at far right. Towle had a planing mill with three planers and the machinery necessary for making laths, doors, sashes, blinds, and moldings. Towle Brothers also had a box manufacturing facility in Sacramento. (Norm Sayler.)

Engine No. 4 has stopped on one of the many trestles built for the Towle Brothers Narrow Gauge Railroad. A lot of timber was used in building the numerous trestles that crossed the many streams on the Towle Brothers property. (AJS.)

A group of men and women poses on a flatcar in front of a Towle Brothers locomotive. This image is from a glass-plate negative, as evidenced by the faint crack in the glass that can be seen running from the bottom of the image right up through the engine's cab. Someone used tape to repair the cracked glass. Sugar pine and ponderosa were the two main species of trees favored by the Towle Brothers Lumber Company. (AJS.)

Steep Hollow Mill was built to process raw logs into rough-cut lumber before transporting it on the Towle Brothers Railroad back to Towle. At Towle, the lumber could be finished in the planing mill and then stacked for seasoning (drying) before being loaded onto Central Pacific flatcars or into boxcars for delivery to retail lumber stores. (Society of California Pioneers.)

Omega Station was near the end of the Towle Brothers narrow-gauge rail line. Omega was a small community across the Bear River in Nevada County. Both images on this page were taken by Charles Beebe Turrill in 1886. His photographs are in various California institutions, such as the Bancroft Library and the Society of California Pioneers. (Society of California Pioneers.)

Most likely this is a view of the Texas Hill logging area and sawmill. This photograph shows a very large swath of property that is being clear-cut. It is hard to determine how large a view this photograph is covering until one realizes that there are train tracks and cordwood cars in the middle of the picture. There is a locomotive in the center of the picture adjacent to the white-roofed building. (AJS.)

To better show the scale of the logging operation seen in this photograph, a zoom-in close-up of the white-roofed building and the locomotive next to it is presented here. (AJS.)

One of the Towle Brothers logging crews is seen here in a posed photograph. An unusual feature of this image is that some of the men are identified on the back of the photograph. In the front row from left to right, the fifth man is Lawrence Beardon; the sixth is Fred Pittman; and the seventh is Jim Johnson. Lawrence Beardon appears in the 1900 federal census for the Alta Precinct as "foreman lumber jack." (AJS.)

A section of a single cut tree trunk is on each flatcar being pulled across one of the many trestles on the Towle Brothers property. The old-growth trees were huge. (AJS.)

This image is of the narrow-gauge caboose. It was abandoned in an open area down behind the Towle Depot. It was pulled out of the weeds and restored and is now on display adjacent to the Dutch Flat Community Center. The caboose had been used as a secure method for delivering the payroll to the men at the remote logging camps and mills. (AJS.)

Towle Brothers expanded its logging operation in the area near Texas Hill. The company also ran a standard-gauge locomotive on a spur track that was connected to the Central Pacific Railroad main line at Fulda. This is Towle Brothers' standard-gauge locomotive No. 25 parked at Fulda, a small community near Emigrant Gap. In 1902, the Towle Brothers Company sold its logging and lumber business to Read Lumber, headquartered in Canada. Prior to that sale, Towle Brothers had shifted most of its operations, including its narrow-gauge railroad, from Towle to the Texas Hill area. (AJS.)

In the Texas Hill area of the logging campaign, the Read Lumber Company built two cable inclines to assist the loaded cars up and down the steep hillside. The incline at right is lowering a carload of cut lumber down the hillside from the sawmill above. In the middle of the tracks, white objects can be seen. These are rollers over which the cable would ride to avoid damaging the wooden ties. At the bottom of the incline, the loaded car was transferred to the narrow-gauge railroad for transport to Fulda. A portion of the straight-line cleared path for this incline is still visible from the Texas Hill Road. (AJS.)

At left is a view of the other steep incline in the Texas Hill logging area. This incline raised carloads of logs to the sawmill at the top of the hill. (AJS.)

A small group of people is being towed to the top of the incline in this photograph. The tow cable can be seen attached to the front of the flatcar. One of the rollers is right in front of the flatcar and is more recognizable for what it is in this photograph. (AJS.)

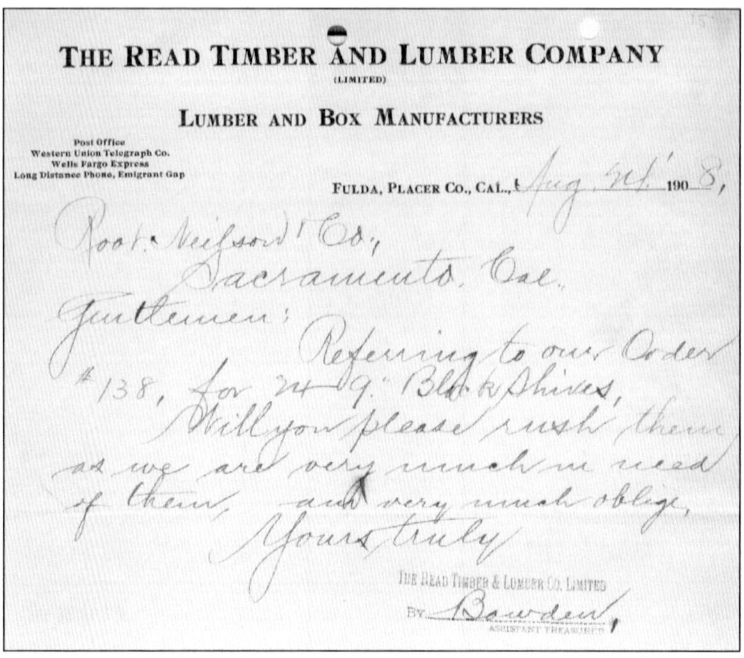

THE READ TIMBER AND LUMBER COMPANY
(LIMITED)
LUMBER AND BOX MANUFACTURERS

Post Office
Western Union Telegraph Co.
Wells Fargo Express
Long Distance Phone, Emigrant Gap

FULDA, PLACER CO., CAL., Aug. 24, 1908,

Root, Neilson & Co.,
Sacramento, Cal.
Gentlemen:
Referring to our Order #138, for 24 - 9" Blk Shives,
Will you please rush them as we are very much in need of them, and very much oblige,
Yours truly

THE READ TIMBER & LUMBER CO. LIMITED
BY Bowden,
ASSISTANT TREASURER

This is a letter to a metal manufacturing company in Sacramento. The letter is dated 1908 and was sent from the Read Lumber Company office at Fulda, Placer County. (AJS.)

Eight

Pacific Gas & Electric Railroads

The San Francisco Gas & Electric Company and the California Gas & Electric Corporation merged in 1905 to form the Pacific Gas & Electric Company (PG&E). In 1906, PG&E purchased the Sacramento Electric, Gas & Railway Company, taking control of its railway operations in and around Sacramento. This got PG&E into the railroad business and established a familiarity with railroad operations. After the merger in 1905, PG&E started expanding its hydroelectric industry through the purchase of existing water storage and conveyance systems throughout the watersheds in Northern California. Placer County was the location for many small dams and flumes left over from the early gold-mining era. PG&E started to utilize these old systems and began to build new facilities geared to increase water storage and to generate electricity from hydroelectric plants built along the fast-flowing rivers.

Around 1912, as the Southern Pacific Railroad was building a second set of tracks up and over the Sierra Nevada and the Mountain Quarries Company was building a railroad near Auburn, PG&E began using part of the old Birce & Smart logging railroad at Lake Spaulding and built a railroad spur at the future site of the Drum Powerhouse near Dutch Flat. The company operated these railroads to aid in the construction of both a larger dam at Lake Spaulding and a new powerhouse on the Bear River. This new powerhouse was named after Frank Drum, who was the president of PG&E from 1907 to 1920.

Francis Albert Birce and Joseph Hutchins Smart formed the Birce & Smart lumber business and built a short-line railroad to haul out felled trees from their extensive holdings in the Yuba River watershed in Nevada County. Their railroad met the Southern Pacific main line railroad at a siding known as Smart in Placer County. Between 1912 and 1914, PG&E assumed control of portions of the Birce & Smart Railroad between the Southern Pacific sidings at Smart and the new Spaulding Dam construction site downstream from the older dam. PG&E was building a larger dam at the Lake Spaulding site and wanted the railroad to facilitate construction efforts. A link between the Towle Brothers and the Birce & Smart logging railroads is the fact that Joseph Hutchins Smart, cofounder of the Birce & Smart lumber business, was once the manager of the pulp and wood mill for Towle Brothers at Towle. The Birce & Smart Railroad used a 300-foot-long, 75-foot-high trestle running across the front of the original Spaulding Dam to reach the Birce & Smart timberlands. The line ran through very rugged country, and portions of the line were built on an eight percent grade, requiring the purchase of a cog-wheel engine, as a regular locomotive could not climb that steep a gradient.

PG&E was also building a power plant down at the bottom of the Bear River canyon as part of the Spaulding-Drum hydroelectric project. Orel was the nearest station on the Southern Pacific main line to the Drum construction site. PG&E built a short-line railroad from Orel to the Drum Powerhouse construction site. The railroad built in support of the construction of the Drum Powerhouse was relatively flat from Orel Station to the top of the Bear River canyon. From the edge of the canyon down to the powerhouse construction site, there was a very steep incline where cables were used to raise and lower the loaded flatcars. These two railroads operated by PG&E in the early part of the 20th century were instrumental in further development of water storage and hydroelectric power generation for Northern California.

The first four images in this chapter are of the Spaulding Lake area near Emigrant Gap. This is a close-up view of the Birce & Smart Railroad trestle running across the face of the original Lake Spaulding Dam. (AJS.)

This image, from an old postcard, shows the Birce & Smart Railroad trestle, the first Lake Spaulding Dam, and Lake Spaulding, which was originally quite small. (AJS.)

The date July 14, 1913, in the lower right corner of this photograph indicates that these tracks descending down to Lake Spaulding are under management of PG&E in its efforts to build a larger dam to increase the holding capacity of Lake Spaulding. (AJS.)

This photograph shows why PG&E wanted to use a railroad at the new Spaulding Dam construction site. Moving the large rocks and construction debris around was much easier with a railway. The connection of this railroad to Southern Pacific's mainline at Smart in Placer County eased bringing heavy equipment down to the construction site. (Ken Yeo.)

This image and the next three are from Drum near Towle. Massive electrical transformers are being transported on flatcars along the spur built by PG&E from the Orel Station on Southern Pacific's main line east of Towle. This part of the spur was built on a flat ridge before descending down the steep incline to the power plant construction site at Drum. (AJS.)

The tracks are descending the incline down to the power plant's construction site. The large sections of pipe would be joined to form the penstocks carrying water from the Drum Reservoir at the top of the hill down to the turbines inside the power plant at the bottom of the incline. The view in the photograph is actually looking west, not east as noted on the image itself. (AJS.)

The steep incline portion of the railway system at Drum can be seen in this photograph of a large piece of electrical generation equipment loaded onto a flatcar being lowered down to the powerhouse construction site. A man can be seen on the uphill side of the loaded flatcar. (Ken Yeo.)

This "speeder" car had its rubber tires removed and replaced with steel railroad wheels, allowing it to use the PG&E spur from Orel to the top of the incline. (AJS.)

Nine

Lake Tahoe Railway & Transportation Company

Duane LeRoy Bliss got his start in the railroad business in 1875, when he built the Lake Tahoe Railroad, which was used to haul wood products from the mills at Glenbrook, Nevada, on the east shore of Lake Tahoe. Bliss saw the beauty of Lake Tahoe and envisioned it becoming a tourist destination. By the 1890s, the decline of the lumber industry was closing Glenbrook's mills, and a mass relocation of the once-bustling east shore community began. The Bliss family, whose extensive business interests had dominated the Glenbrook-area economy, had wisely spared the magnificent stand of trees across the lake, around the lake's outlet at Tahoe City. They began to move the structures and materials to Tahoe City, which would become the basis of their new operations. This new endeavor would emphasize tourism. The Bliss family's plans called for the construction of a hotel to rival any in the country, but preparations necessary for the success of such an undertaking would require the establishment of a comfortable and dependable system of transportation to get tourists from outside to the lake.

To solve the transportation problem, Duane Bliss formed the Lake Tahoe Railway & Transportation Company (L.T. Ry & T. Co.) which built a 16-mile-long, three-foot narrow-gauge railroad that ran from a connection with the Southern Pacific Railroad at Truckee, California, to the waterfront on Lake Tahoe at Tahoe City, California. Duane Leroy Bliss was the founding father of the railway, which opened for business in 1900. The route it took followed the Truckee River, as does the modern State Route 89. The road, the river, and the railroad mirrored each other for most of the way between Truckee in Nevada County and Tahoe City on the shores of Lake Tahoe in Placer County.

At Truckee, the L.T. Ry & T. Co. trains would stop across from the Southern Pacific Railroad depot. Tickets for the Lake Tahoe trains were sold at the east end of the SP depot at a separate ticket office. There was also a separate waiting room inside the SP depot for passengers of the Lake Tahoe trains. Up until the 1930s, the ticket office at the Lake Tahoe terminus was inside the store owned by the Lake Tahoe Mercantile Company. The store had one side facing the pier and the train tracks, while the other side was built on piers right out into Lake Tahoe. Though the train tracks extended all the way to the shop buildings at Tahoe City, the majority of passengers and freight was processed on a long wharf built out into Lake Tahoe below the famous Tahoe Tavern. The role of the Tahoe Tavern in Tahoe City's history is so basic that a discussion of the town's development is incomplete without mention of it. The Tahoe Tavern was built by Duane Bliss to provide a place to stay for the tourists.

Bliss's devotion to Lake Tahoe led him to being responsible for stopping an attempt to lower the rim of Lake Tahoe, which would have lowered the lake level significantly. After Bliss died in 1907, a land development company that had sold property in Nevada planned to again lower the rim of the lake where the Truckee River flows out. The idea was to increase the water flow on the Truckee River to provide irrigation water for the plots of land sold in Nevada. Duane Bliss's son William Bliss went to Washington, DC, in 1915 to argue before the secretary of the interior that lowering the rim of Lake Tahoe at the Truckee River outflow would damage the lake. A third attempt to increase the flow of water on the Truckee River was made in 1920, and again William Bliss made the trip to Washington, DC, to argue against despoiling Lake Tahoe.

The L.T. Ry & T. Co. ran from 1899 until October 16, 1925, when it was leased to the Southern Pacific Company. Southern Pacific bought the property outright in May 1933. After Southern Pacific took over operations in 1925, it converted the system from narrow gauge to standard gauge. Southern Pacific abandoned the Truckee–to–Tahoe City line in 1943. Southern Pacific's justification for ceasing operations was that because of the war effort, vital resources were needed elsewhere, but in truth, the Truckee–to–Lake Tahoe line was not making a profit.

Today, the roadbed of the Lake Tahoe Railway is finding new life as a hiking and biking trail. Portions of the route near Tahoe City have already been converted and are enjoyed by many as they walk or ride along the banks of the Truckee River.

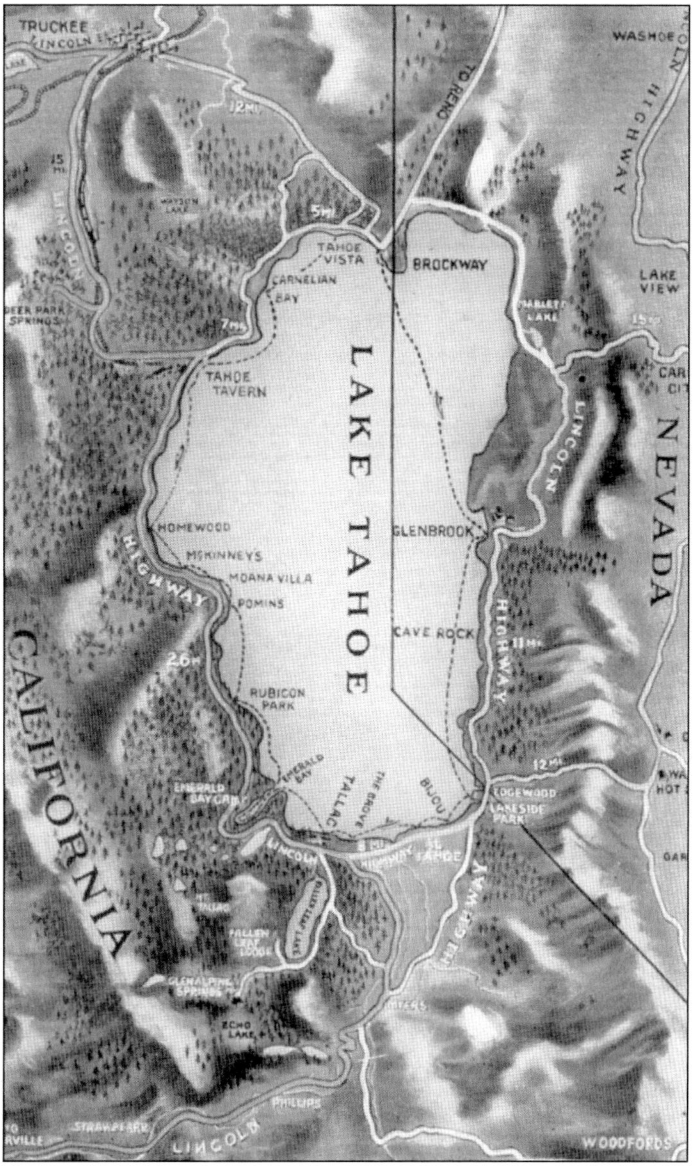

This map is an artist's concept of the Lake Tahoe region and is from an old postcard. The community of Truckee appears in the upper left corner. The Lake Tahoe Railway's tracks, the automobile road, and the Truckee River all appear on the map between Truckee and the Tahoe Tavern. The Truckee River is the sole outlet of Lake Tahoe and flows northeasterly to drain into Pyramid Lake in Nevada. Truckee was the northern terminus for the Lake Tahoe Railway & Transportation Company's railroad. The other end of the Lake Tahoe Railway was at the long wharf extending out into Lake Tahoe from the shoreline at the Tahoe Tavern. Truckee is in Nevada County, while the Tahoe Tavern and most of the Lake Tahoe Railway's tracks were in Placer County. The dotted line seen on the lake depicts the route of the steamships that plied the waters of Lake Tahoe on a regular route and schedule. This map indicates that the Lincoln Highway had an alternate bypass route around both shores of Lake Tahoe, but in reality, it was only on the eastern shore of the lake. The artist mislabeled the road running along the western shore as also being the Lincoln Highway. (AJS.)

An early photograph of the outskirts of Truckee shows two railroad lines entering the town from the west. The tracks on the left are Southern Pacific's main line tracks. The tracks at the far right, passing under the water tower, are the Lake Tahoe Railway's narrow-gauge tracks. (Dana Scanlon.)

A Lake Tahoe Railway train is ready to head south to Lake Tahoe. The two-story building in the background is the Southern Pacific Railroad Hotel, and the one-story building to the far left is the train depot used by both the Southern Pacific Railroad and the Lake Tahoe Railway companies. (Dana Scanlon.)

Locomotive No. 3 of the Lake Tahoe Railway and Transportation Company is at Truckee. (Dana Scanlon.)

As mentioned in this chapter's introduction, the routes of an automobile road, the Truckee River, and the Lake Tahoe Railway's tracks mirrored each other the entire distance between the town of Truckee in the north and Lake Tahoe in the south. This image shows all three side by side. (AJS.)

At the Lake Tahoe end of the railroad's route was the wharf extending out into Lake Tahoe. The majority of time, the trains would turn and back onto the wharf, as seen here. People are walking off the pier up to the Tahoe Tavern. A steamship is tied up at the wharf ready to take on passengers. (AJS.)

Another view of the wharf was taken from one of the lake's steamships. A train is turned and headed north for a return trip to Truckee. At the head end of the pier on the left is the casino building adjacent to the Tahoe Tavern hotel. (Dana Scanlon.)

In this image, a Lake Tahoe Railway train is coming off the wharf heading back to Truckee. (Tony Hesch.)

Lake Tahoe Railway locomotive No. 1 is en route between Truckee and Lake Tahoe. All of the railroad's rolling stock was originally sized for the narrow-gauge tracks. When Southern Pacific took over operations in 1925, it converted the narrow-gauge tracks to standard gauge and replaced all of the narrow-gauge equipment with standard-gauge locomotives and railcars. (AJS.)

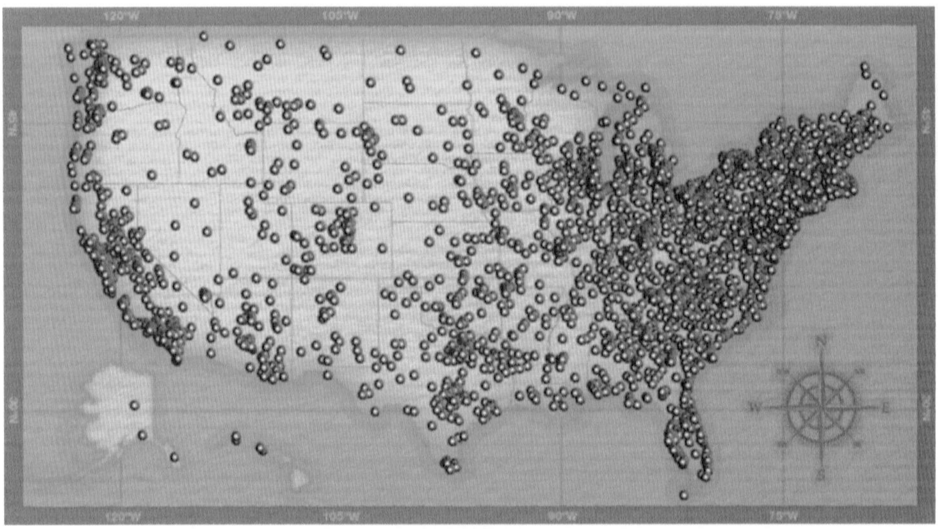